INTRODUCING AND MANAGING ACADEMIC LIBRARY AUTOMATION PROJECTS

Recent Titles in
The Greenwood Library Management Collection

Introducing and Managing Academic Library Automation Projects

Edited by
John W. Head and Gerard B. McCabe

THE GREENWOOD LIBRARY MANAGEMENT COLLECTION

GREENWOOD PRESS
Westport, Connecticut • London

Library of Congress Cataloging-in-Publication Data

Introducing and managing academic library automation projects / edited
   by John W. Head and Gerard B. McCabe.
      p.   cm.—(The Greenwood library management collection ; ISSN
0894–2986)
   Includes bibliographical references (p.   )and index.
   ISBN 0–313–29633–2 (alk. paper)
   1. Academic libraries—United States—Data processing.
   2. Academic libraries—United States—Automation.   I. Head, John W.
II. McCabe, Gerard B.   III. Series.
Z675.U5I597   1996
027.7'0285—dc20   95–46421

British Library Cataloguing in Publication Data is available.

Library of Congress Catalog Card Number: 95–46421
ISBN: 0–313–29633–2
ISSN: 0894–2986

First published in 1996

Greenwood Press, 88 Post Road West, Westport, CT 06881
An imprint of Greenwood Publishing Group, Inc.

Printed in the United States of America

The paper used in this book complies with the
Permanent Paper Standard issued by the National
Information Standards Organization (Z39.48–1984).

10 9 8 7 6 5 4 3 2 1

Contents

II. Technical Services in Academic Libraries

III. Keeping Up with Library Automation

Preface

John W. Head

When Gerry McCabe and I finished editing *The Insider's Guide to Library Automation*, we discussed the possible usefulness of another, different kind of book about library automation. Our earlier book was, as planned, a group of chapters by librarians describing in detail the automation projects they knew best—their own. We asked them to describe those experiences at a level of detail, including troubles, often lacking in published accounts of library automation. We purposely sought to include librarians who were new authors. For our second book together, we decided to follow many of the same approaches, but to shift the focus from detailed accounts of automation projects to the management of library automation. Again we sought to include new authors, and we wanted many of our authors to be able to describe their own administrative experiences.

We were very pleased with the efforts of our *Insider's Guide* authors, and we are pleased with the efforts of our new group of authors. Technical details have not vanished. We still have detailed accounts of library automation projects, but the emphasis is less on the technical details, and more on the forecasting, planning, implementing, and monitoring necessary for the successful management of library automation. As a result, this book will be a valuable professional reference for academic librarians.

Introduction

Gerard B. McCabe

In June 1995, librarians and support staff members of Clarion University Libraries attended an all day workshop at the Pittsburgh Regional Library Center. The purpose was to allow the attendees an opportunity to hear librarians who work with various online systems discourse on their experience. Clarion staff are involved in a project to develop a proposal for a new online system to replace the eight-year-old system that is in use. The Clarion people were surprised to hear several attendees from other academic libraries mention the lack of automation of any kind. This is not unusual at all. The editors are well aware that a fair number of academic libraries still lack an online system of any kind. This book is not intended for the novice, or for librarians who are working in libraries that are card catalog–based. We hope such people will read this book, but our intended audience is the library and its staff that either has or is developing additional offline or online automated systems for service to the library's public.

In the opening paragraph of the preface to our 1993 book, *Insider's Guide to Library Automation*, we commented on the large number of libraries that were lacking online catalogs. We learned this through telephone calls to the major regional networks. Apparently, little has changed in the past three years.

The authors of this book's chapters come from all types of academic libraries and our intent, while offering a variety of experiences, is to focus on two major areas: public service—providing information—and technical services (especially catalog departments)—preparing and organizing the databases used in public services, first the online catalog and secondly supplementary databases.

The traditional role of the catalog department is the organization of the collections, and in effect the organization of knowledge into easily retrievable segments. It is only natural for professional peers to look to the catalog department to organize the locally developed databases that are produced in the library and other campus offices for placement on the online system. Beyond the local needs looms the Internet, and the forthcoming National Research and Education Network (NREN) with the National Information Infrastructure (NII). The Internet, already deplored as uncontrolled, with a mishmash of assorted information sources, appears to offer little sense of organization. If the NII is to become a reality and be useful in a meaningful way to American society at large, it must begin with organization—sensible, logical arrangements of the information databases it will contain—and this issue falls to the purview of the skilled cataloger.

Themes that run consistently through many of these chapters are planning, teamwork, and understanding of objectives. Any work effort involving automation requires very careful planning. The costs of any automated project are very high; the equipment is expensive; the software is expensive, but usually challenging as well. It is pointless to begin a project of any magnitude without a well-thought-out plan, which should include provisions for coordinating related activities or events that must occur as the project develops, as well as possible contingency actions if missteps occur. All people involved must know the plan, their role in it, and how to work together so that the outcome is never in doubt. Our authors bring this message home frequently in their narratives. Automation projects are never easy. Mental concentration, much advance planning, reading of literature, visits to other more advanced libraries, consultation with colleagues, use of consultants in some instances, and vendor specialists— all can be part of the project.

Each of the three parts of this book begins with an introduction that briefly summarizes its theme and the topic of each chapter. Part I concerns public services in academic libraries, particularly with online and offline automated information services. Part II covers technical services, especially the organization of the library's principal database, the online catalog. Part III consists of four chapters: one setting out means of organizing for automation; another dealing with the library building; the other two are bibliographic essays.

The editors hope this book will be useful to librarians, library administrators, and library and information science students.

The editors acknowledge the assistance of Peggy Postlewait, library administrative secretary, and Barbara Reed, administrative secretary of the Department of Library Science, Clarion University of Pennsylvania.

INTRODUCING AND MANAGING ACADEMIC LIBRARY AUTOMATION PROJECTS

PART I

Public Services in Academic Libraries

The five chapters in Part I of this book deal with the changes that automation has brought to libraries, and how librarians can manage this change to provide good services. While the six chapters in Part II deal mainly with technical services and database maintenance, these chapters deal mainly with providing services to readers.

In Chapter 1, Paul F. Burton provides an overview of library automation, its impact on libraries as institutions and librarians as professionals, and the changes it has made in the nature of library work. He explains that the first round of organizational change as a consequence of automation will inevitably be followed by further changes, and that librarians must manage change well to produce good services. Mr. Burton skillfully reviews a key portion of the literature dealing with the management of automation and how automation has and will change libraries and the work of librarians and other library staff.

The remaining four chapters all deal with one of the most significant technological changes that librarians must learn to work with and to use successfully. This is the technology of networks, especially local area networks (LANs), but larger networks as well. LANs provide many functions that were lacking in early library automation systems. They allow distributed computer power so that complex systems can operate on microcomputers. Since microcomputers are typically much less expensive than larger computers, costs may be less, even though several computers have replaced a single computer connected to terminals. Since each microcomputer in the network has processing power, the loss of one computer may not stop all functions at once; indeed, the loss of one computer may hardly be noticed. Networks also allow communications, the capability of running many kinds of software, and the interconnection of different kinds of computers.

While networks have many advantages, they force librarians to learn a complex new layer of technology. They present us with a wonderful variety of options, some very attractive and powerful. Using LANs and wide area networks (WANs), we can do all kinds of things we couldn't do before. The choices, however, are complex; making good choices isn't easy. There are many ways of doing the same thing and each way has different capabilities and costs. Furthermore, networks are frequently expensive to build, to maintain, and to repair when they fail.

Clearly, most people working in library automation believe that networks are an improvement and that networked local automation systems will replace the old minicomputer (or mainframe) linked to simple computer terminals. Most people believe the advantages make networks the means we should choose for the next round of library automation. This change is already underway in local automation systems, shared automation systems, and in providing access to databases. These ideas and problems are a common theme in the following four chapters.

Chapter 2, by Melanie J. Norton, and Chapter 3, by Terrence F. Mech, Judith Tierney, and Jennifer L. Walz, complement each other well. Ms. Norton's chapter is an extensive, well-documented overview of LANs in libraries, while Terry Mech and his coauthors have done an excellent job of documenting the building and evolution of a specific library LAN.

In Chapter 4, Tom Klingler and Rick Wiggins describe the management of the campus-wide local information service they developed at The University of Akron. This chapter is especially strong on the politics of and training requirements for a large cooperative information system with many information providers.

In Chapter 5, Margaret Sylvia deals with a major reader services problem almost wholly new to librarians. This is the problem of accessing bibliographic databases and full-text via several methods—a set of choices that is largely new to us. Local access to mainly bibliographic databases on CD-ROM has been commonplace since the mid-1980s; locally loaded or mounted databases became more widely used by several larger academic libraries by the late 1980s (very few such systems had been installed earlier in academic libraries); the 1990s seems to be the decade of full-text databases. Ms. Sylvia helps us thread our way through the choices of print, CD-ROM, locally loaded, and remote online access for both full-text and bibliographic databases. While this is clearly an opportunity, it is also a real problem because of the many permutations in access methods and in costs.

1

Automation: Changing the Structure of Library and Information Services

Paul F. Burton

While much has been said and written about the applications of library automation and the processes of design and implementation, the question of how this automation affects the management and structure of library and information services (LIS) has received less attention. This need not be unduly surprising, since the impact on organizational structure is not as well understood as the systems design process, and the presence of contingency factors unique to each organization often make generalizations difficult.

What we do know is that the technology itself is an essentially neutral agent in the change process, and that management attitudes and philosophy therefore play the most important part in determining what, if any, changes can be made to organizational structures. The flexibility of automated systems means that managements can choose to use them in ways that accord with their wishes: technology can help to increase or decrease centralized control; it can give staff greater or lesser control over the flow of their work; it can be used to increase variety, flexibility, and skills levels or to "Taylorize" work to an even greater extent by reducing operations to the smallest component possible (Zuboff 1988).

Despite a lack of certainty, the ways in which automation affects organizational structures is an important topic, for LIS must consider not only how to put technology to the best use, but also how to change structures to maximize the benefits to their users. Having introduced automated procedures, organizations appear to go through a series of phases in its use: first comes the automation of the routine work, such as circulation control, for example. This then frees staff to deal with other aspects of the service that were less well handled because of the demands of the routine, and at this stage LIS (along with other organizations) can begin to examine the possibilities for an extension of the service provided. Once this is under way, LIS managers can examine the possibilities for changes to the organizational structure and workflow, a process that may involve creating new supervisory levels and moving staff from one service area to another. There are differing views over how this can be translated into an organizational "picture." It may result in an increase in the number of middle managers supervising a reduced number of nonprofessional staff (the routine tasks being now automated), or in flatter hierarchies in which more professional work is carried out by paraprofessionals, with fewer professionals being used to deal with those tasks outside the competencies of the paraprofessionals. In addition, the professionals may move away from technical services, such as cataloging and classification, and take up an increased intermediary role between information resources (especially, but not exclusively, the networked resources). While automation obviously has a major role in reducing the routine work of LIS staff, it also provides (or should provide) numerous other opportunities further "up stream" in the flow from information creator to information user.

This in turn has major implications for staffing and professional education: automation can mean one-third fewer staff and a reduced number of work activities (Dehennin 1988), enabling professional staff to move to "front of house" activities in direct contact with patrons (Burton 1990). A different set of skills is then required of the professional, namely, the ability to communicate with LIS patrons, to understand their information needs, and to use a range of resources to meet those needs.

If there is a lesson to be learned from the application of automation in other organizations, it is that automating the routine work is only the start of a change process that will ultimately affect the entire organization. It is all the more important, therefore, to be aware of this and to plan for it from the start. Automation can be introduced as part of a strategic plan based on a user-centered philosophy of information provision, rather than on an ad hoc basis, thus minimizing disruption and the adverse effects on staff. Change is unsettling for everyone, and it seems that change caused by automation is particularly unsettling, with a wide range of concerns being expressed. Planning from the start is a way to reduce that friction and to deal with staff concerns; another is by involving staff in the entire process from design to implementation, and many methodologies now exist to incorporate staff participation (Jackson 1991).

The need to change is made all the more urgent by the rise of competitors in information provision who use the self-same technology, often on a commercial basis, and the development of networked information resources via the Internet, which, in theory at least, can be accessed by anyone with the appropriate equipment without the need for an intermediary service. If LIS do not restructure to gain the maximum benefit from automation, including the provision of online information resources, they run the risk of being sidelined by newer offerings.

Though the free-or-fee argument is outside the scope of this chapter, it has to be recognized that large sections of the community will pay for accurate information, delivered on time in the form required. LIS no longer have a monopoly on information provision and, with a greater range of information providers to choose from (for some sections of the population, at least), information users are becoming more discerning in their demands. More than one librarian has warned recently of the threat to LIS if they do not seize the opportunities provided by automation: more positively, it has been asked, "What value does the library add? . . . We must move beyond the card catalog to a navigation aid that assists scholars in moving through their intellectual universe" (van Houwelin 1994: 10).

Traditionally, we can say that LIS have organized collections of documents in ways that, in theory at least, have aided retrieval from a variety of sources. The value added by LIS has been in cataloging, to provide a uniform record of a document, and in classification, to provide a subject arrangement and finding tool. Information needs were met primarily (though not, of course, exclusively) by the collection, augmented as required by interlibrary lending. Not surprisingly, this approach, though valid for the concept of a document collection, meant that emphasis was placed on the skills of the cataloger and classifier. With the growth of electronic information resources that may be located anywhere in the world and that do not have to be physically present in the LIS building, the philosophy is now one of access to information, rather than custody of documents: the LIS becomes a window (or better, a doorway) onto information that can be retrieved as required. It has become a cliché to speak of "just in time" information provision replacing "just in case" information storage.

However, this conflicts with the traditional notions of the collection and organization of material through cataloging and classification. These professional skills become less central to the service (especially with growth of shared cataloging systems), and are replaced by at least a basic technical knowledge of computer systems and (more importantly still) by knowledge and understanding of the networked information resources, a task made difficult by the rapidly changing nature of these resources. The LIS professional must know these resources as well as he or she knows (or once knew) printed reference sources and must be able to use them in the service of the patron, with the added complication that electronic resources, though theoretically more current, are also less stable than printed resources. The added value here is understanding of the structure of networked resources and the ability to evaluate them in the light of the patron's needs.

LIS managers, therefore, must be aware of the potential for structural change in their services and how to cope with it, just as their counterparts in the commercial sector have recognized the need for new workflows and structures (Evald 1992: 163). Simply replacing manual routines with automated ones will not extract the maximum benefit from automation. As we have already sug-

gested, the possibilities—using the parallel of organizations in other sectors—
are flatter hierarchies in which there are fewer professional staff in middle grades
and a higher degree of semiprofessional work carried out by paraprofessional
staff, and/or more flexible structures that adapt to the rapidly changing information environment within which LIS operate and that is now populated with
many other providers. Providing access to information means increased face-to-
face contact with patrons and, as was suggested earlier, this is facilitated by
automation. Old structures based on processing the flow of documents are no
longer relevant, and this means that LIS managers must reexamine the existing
divisions into technical services, public services, and so on. At its most extreme,
changing structures may involve merging with another unit: this has become
commonplace in the United Kingdom (UK), where many university libraries
have merged with the university's computer center to form a new information
services department, often with the former librarian in charge of a very different
service built around access through technology. Another example is that of Tilburg University in the Netherlands, where a specific plan has been launched to
create a "modern information and study center" that will provide

facilities to optimize the searching process in that explosively growing amount of information. For this, knowledge navigation systems have to be developed that are easy to
use for researchers, teachers, and students. This will also require an integration of librarian applications with other computer applications that are important for the primary
process. (Geleijnse and Grootaers 1994: vii)

Managers must also be aware, however, that the impact of automation will
differ for the various grades of personnel within the service. It is important to
note that, in an essentially conservative profession, many of these changes will
be resisted to a greater or lesser degree: we will see some sign of this later in
this chapter. There is evidence to suggest that, for some staffing levels at least,
automation is a source of increased job satisfaction: Waters has found that clerical staff report improved flexibility and creativity in the work done (1986,
1988), and Lynch and Verdin (1987) report higher levels of job satisfaction
among reference personnel than among those working in any other area. Similarly, the majority of library support staff experience increased job satisfaction
following automation and feel that they are more effective (Palmini 1994: 123).
However, LIS staff are no more immune to concerns over automation than any
other service: personnel are concerned about job losses, the effect on social
relationships at work, and health and safety. In a study of Canadian libraries,
Dakshinamurti found significant numbers of people expressing concern over loss
of interpersonal communication and feelings about insecurity and insignificance
(1985: 348), while a survey of UK public libraries found suggestions that the
introduction of automation had created more work for some staff, because the
system's effectiveness made it possible to carry out tasks not previously considered feasible (Craghill, Neale, and Wilson 1989: 17). LIS managers must

therefore be capable of introducing and managing change successfully, using participative decision making, communication skills, and understanding.

Furthermore, there is a need to appreciate that restructuring does not just happen. It must be a conscious decision that is incorporated into a strategic plan for the LIS: only this way can maximum benefit be derived with minimum adverse effect on personnel and service quality. An excellent example of this process, along with instances of restructuring and changing workflow, is afforded by Pennsylvania State University Library, which developed a strategic plan built around its move to shared cataloging (Bednar 1988). As a case study, it exemplifies a great deal of what can and should be done.

The entire operation was, first of all, based on an explicit plan that included reorganization, redesign of the workflow involved in cataloging procedures, and a resulting change in the roles of personnel (Bednar 1988: 145). Penn State therefore introduced two new sections: bibliographic processing, for copy cataloging and pre-order searching; and cataloging, to which section all professional and paraprofessional catalogers were moved from previously separate sections. All acquisitions became part of a unified workflow, with separation of basic clerical routines from those materials that need professional or paraprofessional judgment.

The new bibliographic processing section was able to deal with 97 percent of all titles using shared cataloging (Bednar 1988: 148). The remaining 3 percent of complex cataloging problems, often in foreign languages, were referred to the cataloging section and its professionals or paraprofessionals. Paraprofessionals were used to supervise clerical staff, representing a major change in their job functions; while, in addition to developing subject headings and maintaining authority files, the professionals were brought out of the "back room" into liaison with public services, thus placing them in more direct contact with library patrons. This was facilitated by a reduction in the staffing levels needed for professional cataloging and the absorption of these posts into other areas of the library (Bednar 1988: 147). The reduction in overall staffing numbers, combined with an increase in the number of titles processed annually, was achieved by natural attrition, though it is not clear which posts (professional or nonprofessional) were lost in this way.

Also part of the plan was the concept of speedy service to patrons, here taking the form of rapid processing of new material rather than a concern for perfect cataloging, but we should note that the majority of patrons were satisfied with the new system. It had become an effective finding tool, which was their main criterion for judging the library: patrons have little appreciation of the minutiae of cataloging and classification if it means a delay in obtaining new material. Nor is this an isolated instance of improvement: it has been found in other libraries, though there was also evidence that the catalogers took the opposite view and gradually reimposed the earlier standards of cataloging (von Cotta Schonberg 1989: 52). There must be a note of caution, however: while Penn State and a few others may stand as examples of what can be done, it seems that they are, for the moment, relatively unusual: "The responding libraries indicated overwhelmingly that technical services and public services divisions will not be added to anyone's endangered species list very soon" (Larsen 1991: 79).

Why this should be so is not entirely clear, though conservatism must be a major factor, as we saw with the move back toward perfect cataloging at the expense of processing speed. There is also the risk that catalogers are allowing their concern for professional levels of processing to displace the concept of service to users. Their immediate interest is in the organization of a collection of documents, but the demand is for access to and exploitation of the information those documents contain. This genuine concern for the maintenance of professional standards is entirely understandable, and a result of decades of education and training that emphasized knowledge and understanding of the cataloging codes and classification schemes required to organize collections of documents.

Such knowledge and understanding is, however, a requirement of the older philosophy of collection maintenance and organization; it is not the basis for a service providing access to, and mediation of, information in numerous formats, including electronic. This type of service requires personnel capable of acting as intermediaries between information and patron, intermediaries who are familiar with technology and possess communication skills, and this means a change in the already crowded curriculum designed to produce LIS professionals. It is unlikely that cataloging and classification, as curriculum subjects, will disappear in the immediate future, but they have to take their place alongside newer topics, such as networked information resources and communication skills. Such changes have, of course, already been introduced into many schools of library and information studies, but it will take time for the new generation of graduates to move through the ranks of the profession to a point where they will have an effect on structures. In the meantime, existing LIS managers must grasp the nettle, and many have done so.

The need to concentrate on access, with all that implies for structures and the deployment of staffing, is particularly acute when we consider the growth of electronic information resources exemplified by the Internet. While these resources are accessible to the user with the relevant equipment, they can be intimidating and difficult to use effectively. As the virtual library concept develops, the question of the organization of documents obviously becomes less pressing, being replaced by the need for knowledge of changing resources, which are more varied in nature, less permanent, and often of more varied quality. Thus, the information professional needs not only an ability to find information in the vast web of the Internet, but also the skills to judge its provenance: Where does it originate? What are the credentials of the provider? What procedures are in place to ensure currency and accuracy? These are not necessarily qualities the typical net surfer will acquire, giving the intermediary an even more important place in the information chain, especially since questions are raised from time to time about the overall quality, accuracy, and currency of resources provided over a network for which there is no central controlling body. (The Australian National University has developed a World Wide Web page to act as focal point for issues of, and suggestions for, maintaining and improving the quality of networked information, though this concentrates largely on standards for presentation [The Australian National University].)

Similarly, LIS must be able to provide these resources (as most academic and many public libraries do) in the full knowledge that they are less amenable to the application of cataloging and classification rules. It is impossible to fix these electronic resources in time: the best that can be done (and it is a lot) is to know how to use them to the best advantage of the patron, but the knowledge of what is there and how to retrieve it will exist largely in the heads of LIS staff, rather than on machine readable catalog records. Some LIS are maintaining "databases" of Internet addresses and World Wide Web Uniform Resource Locations (URLs) or incorporating them into Web browser booklists, but this is a far cry from applying AACR2. On the other hand, it is becoming imperative that LIS consider ways in which these electronic resources can be listed in some form that is accessible by patrons, and the possibility exists for Online Public Access Catalogs (OPACs) to contain built-in links to Internet gopher, ftp, and Web sites. This would suggest that LIS will have to assign some form of indexing to these sites, so that patrons can retrieve them with standard subject searches of OPAC, along with references to documents in the LIS collection. While there is no suggestion that Internet resources and the like will replace printed material in the immediate future, it is the case that patrons will expect LIS to provide access to them. The most likely scenario is similar to that for online searching of database hosts—the end user will search for material he or she knows is available, but will require a trained intermediary for more detailed searching and retrieval.

In conclusion, this chapter has tried to show that LIS must look carefully at the implications of automation for organizational structures, in order to maximize the benefits to be derived. Simple automation (mechanization would be more appropriate) of routine tasks is not sufficient, nor is it likely that LIS will be able to stop there. Elimination or reduction of the routine aspects of LIS work provides an opportunity to move staff to work that should be more satisfying and indeed challenging; this move brings with it the imperative for new structures that integrate workflow and allow staff to serve information needs rather than collection maintenance.

REFERENCES

The Australian National University. Coombs Computing Unit. "Quality Guidelines & Standards for Internet Information Resources" (available from URL: http://coombs.anu.edu.au/SpecialProj/QLTY/QltyHome.html).

Bednar, M. 1988. "Automation of Cataloguing: Effects on Use of Staff, Efficiency and Service to Patrons." *Journal of Academic Librarianship* 14: 145–159.

Burton, P.F. 1990. "Accuracy of Information Provision: The Need for Client-Centred Service." *Journal of Librarianship* 22: 201–215.

Craghill, D., C. Neale, and T.D. Wilson. 1989. *The Impact of IT on Staff Deployment in UK Public Libraries.* London: British Library (British Library Research paper 69).

Dakshinamurti, G. 1985. "Automation's Effect on Library Personnel." *Canadian Library Journal* 42: 343–351.

Dehennin, W. 1988. "Aspects of Organization in a Computerised Library." *Library Bulletin* 21: 117–130.

Evald, P. 1992. "Organizational Development in Danish Public Libraries: Computer Mediated Work and Strategic Vision." *Journal of Librarianship and Information Science* 24: 159–168.

Geleijnse, H., and C. Grootaers (eds). 1994. *Developing the Library of the Future: The Tilburg Experience.* Tilburg: Tilburg University Press.

Jackson, M. 1991. *Systems Methodology for the Management Sciences.* New York and London: Plenum.

Larsen, P.M. 1991. "The Climate of Change: Library Organizational Structures, 1985–1990." In *Access Services: The Convergence of Reference and Technical Services*, ed. G.M. McCombs. New York and London: Haworth Press, pp. 79–93.

Lynch, B.P., and J.A. Verdin. 1987. "Job Satisfaction in Libraries: A Replication." *Library Quarterly* 57: 190–202, quoted in J.B. Whitlach (1991), "Automation and Job Satisfaction Among Reference Librarians." *Computers in Libraries* 11: 32–34.

Palmini, C.C. 1994. "The Impact of Computerization on Library Support Staff: A Study of Support Staff in Academic Libraries in Wisconsin." *College and Research Libraries* 55: 119–127.

van Houwelin, D.E. 1994. "Knowledge Services in the Digitized World: Possibilities and Strategies." In *Electronic Access to Information: A New Service Paradigm*, eds. W.S.S. Chiang and N.E. Elkington. Proceedings from the symposium held July 23–24, 1993, Palo Alto, California. Mountain View, Calif.: Research Libraries Group, pp. 5–16.

von Cotta Schonberg, M. 1989. "Automation and Academic Library Structure." *Libri* 39: 47–63.

Waters, D. 1986. "Assessing the Impact of New Technology on Library Employees." *LASIE* 17: 20–27.

———. 1988. "New Technology and Job Satisfaction in University Libraries." *LASIE* 18: 103–108.

Zuboff, S. 1988. *In the Age of the Smart Machine: The Future of Work and Power.* Oxford: Heinemann.

2

Local Area Networks in Brief

Melanie J. Norton

INTRODUCTION

Decreasing costs of microcomputers, coupled with significant increases in storage capacity, memory, speed, and versatility, are contributing to the increased prevalence of local area networks (LANs). Networked computer systems are installed in virtually every sphere of business, academic, and nonprofit environments. LAN systems provide communication links within offices and, by connecting LANs, throughout buildings, across campuses, even around the world. Beyond basic communications, LANs provide resource sharing of hardware, software, and information (Madron 1994).

Reliance on these devices and systems is so great that estimates of the productivity losses caused by LAN operation failures for just one major corporation may exceed three million dollars per year. On average, one-half business day per month is lost due to LAN failure or service disruption (Dauber 1991). Whether those lost days occur at a major manufacturing site or small business office, they translate into significant direct economic losses in productivity (Dauber 1991). When library networks are down, there are direct and indirect costs to the library and its patrons. Library management tasks, as well as technical activities, are halted and patron access to local online catalogs or external network connections stops. All the wonderment of automation ceases, reminding library staff that machines can and do "break." Frequently, automation failures are the result of management failures. There are multiple aspects to management of automation that contribute to the success or failure of automation. Management of hardware and software, at minimum, requires a completed systems analysis, availability and creation of documentation (including operational procedures), awareness of system limitations, and sensitivity to user requirements. Constant reevaluation of systems, human and machine, is also necessary in light of ever-changing technology. The complexity of environments supported by automation necessitate a corresponding sophistication of management. Libraries are an example of an extraordinarily complex environment. The activities of the library: collection, acquisitions, cataloging and classification, reference, and serials service—ultimately the access and retrieval of information—are complex endeavors. Providing appropriate automation management, especially LAN management, demands attention to all the complications of the library mission. Automation in libraries must serve technical needs of professionals handling the collection, as well as serve various skill levels and needs of library patrons. This is a two-fold problem, as expectations of librarians are quite different than those of most patrons, in any library setting.

Automation of libraries has been an ongoing process for several decades. Like most other enterprises engaging in automation efforts, libraries have been and still are undergoing changes previously unimagined due entirely to the impact of automation on virtually every information task. Librarians and library staff have contributed to developing protocols for data sharing, machine-readable format, portions of the Internet, and many other aspects of automation. The need for improved management techniques and managers accelerates as library facilities develop or expand their application of, and reliance on, both computer and networking technology. Speed of technological changes in computing and networking has propelled the proliferation of LANs, as well as hardware and software tools to supervise and monitor most technical aspects of LANs. Technological haste has also contributed to management being handled by people who may not have the technological training associated with computers or networks. Though librarians are practically and conceptually educated in the management of information, the transition to including computers and networks as tools in this task presents a continuing technological challenge.

Fundamental to all automation is the function of management, but LAN management is still a developing art. Historically, management of LAN systems has fallen to ''ad hoc administrators who acquire their skills on the fly, learning to deal with new demands as they arise. As enterprise-wide LANs materialize, that approach won't remain viable'' (Sloman 1991: 175). ''An effective network control center depends on the acumen of human operators . . . and most [organizations] aren't paying nearly enough attention to selecting and training this critical personnel'' (Barnhart 1992: 138). In fact, ''network management is as much a black art as a science'' (Ryan 1991: 155).

Keeping track of technology is not the same as managing systems. Users, documentation, and planning for the future must be accepted components of network management (Udell 1991). Merely keeping these information tools running is not enough, LANs as resources must be controlled, and growth must be monitored to meet the needs and complexity of the facility. Since computer systems in libraries serve multiple-user populations in a variety of areas—technical services, circulation, reference, serials, administration, and public access catalogs—the systems must be flexible. Their design and maintenance should involve the expertise not only of computer specialists, but also the professional information management skills of the various librarians, as well as someone representing the average library patron.

Many existing computer systems may not be providing the level of productivity or efficiency for any of the users that was forecast. Focusing on more concepts and methodologies from library and information science will contribute managerial tools to LANs. Woodsworth (1991) points out that experience with automation in general demonstrates the necessity of information and computing professionals to work together to address the successful implementation of information technology. Information management, rather than just technology management, will contribute to the management of LANs. A team effort to integrate the technical skills of computer specialists with the information management skills of librarians is the most direct solution to a variety of computer system problems. While some may consider this paramount to opening Pandora's box, there may be no other rational alternative. Team management of resources does not mean one vote per team member; there is still a leader, a decision maker who works to keep in balance the technological requirements and information accessibility of the system. Team management, however, will contribute to a growth of knowledge as technical skills become less mysterious and information management becomes better understood. Balancing hardware and software requirements with the need to provide services to a diverse clientele, which includes the providers of the services, is not a small task.

Automation's impact on our society has changed the way people communicate, and changed what patrons want or even expect from libraries. New services to entice the public and to serve the library audience are being based on automation. The success of the Blacksburg, Virginia, electronic village, which has a library as a key provider of Internet access, is but one outstanding example (Helm 1994). The changing role of libraries in schools into proactive resource and multimedia centers with Internet access is another example (McKenzie 1995). These efforts require the expertise of many people, with many points of view and many visions. The success of future automation efforts demands cooperation, communication, documentation, and collaborative efforts.

FEATURES AND MANAGEMENT

Organization

Simplistically, LANs are tools primarily used for sharing resources, especially information. LANs rely on being able to communicate among computers to share resources of a central computer, and now via wider area links, to share resources of remote computers. LANs, then, are resource storage and communication tools. Beyond storage, they also tend to become depositories and distribution sites of information in various stages of formation (McClure et al. 1991: ch. 6). LANs become limited "information centers," though not in the traditional sense that Lancaster described (1979: 1–14). With the fast growth of networking technology, little time has been given to establishing "acquisition and storage policies . . . and a guaranteed source of access" (Lancaster 1979: 3). LANs do not "organize and control . . . by cataloging, classification, indexing and related procedures" per se, as Lancaster suggests are the mark of information centers (1979: 3). To be able to access and share resources, including information, there must be organization. LANs use a variety of organizational techniques to control and access these resources.

The initial organizational feature is the file system within a file server, the primary computer of the network. A file server is divided into volumes that are then divided into directories, which may be divided into subdirectories. The least item in the hierarchy is the file, or document (Novell 1991a). This structure is common to microcomputers, file cabinets, and various other storage and retrieval systems. The structure is also a primary step in the hierarchical, or even relational, classification of data, or information.

The file server's structure may be protected by assigning rights and controlling access based on the requirements and skill levels of users. Using rights to protect the file server is a common and recommended method to ensure resource integrity as well as user privacy. Rights and access control are attached to each user's account. Rights and access restrictions determine which parts of the file server a user may enter and how resources may be used by that account. Failure to assign sufficient rights for users can make the network unusable. Assigning too many rights can undermine the entire structure of the network. Therefore, assigning too few or too many rights can create situations that result in total system failure (Novell 1991a).

The assignment of rights, access control, and directory structure design generally falls to a person fulfilling the role of network manager. As previously mentioned, this person often is not specifically trained in the management of the network software or hardware, or even in the management of information in general. This kind of situation sometimes contributes to an inappropriate LAN organization and structure.

Location of software files and related organization is critical to the proper functioning of the server. Software packages must be in directories that allow user access but do not allow a user to modify the executable code of the software package. Placement of the executable files and temporary user files, as well as ensuring user control over these files, can be critical to the proper performance of the software as well as the network. Accessibility of files within the system, whether in shared directories or in personal directories, should be monitored to ensure maximum user access, file server efficiency, and resource protection (Novell 1991a, 1991b).

A library LAN provides access to the shared database(s) that contain the bibliographic records of the collection, the acquisitions trail, the circulation records, an OPAC, and possibly some unrelated support software. Two specific user groups would rely on such a system: the library staff handling the input and management of bibliographic records, and the library patrons who access the system only for retrieval purposes. These different user groups would require different levels of access and security rights.

System Analysis

A system analysis should be undertaken when the library first considers any form of automation. At that time, and periodically thereafter, all aspects of operations should be completely evaluated, documented, and examined. Prior to making any automation decisions, clearly identify and document the operation, activity, procedures, and rationale for actions. Demographics of all user populations should also be collected and evaluated. Give specific attention to the differences in user population needs. The information that the library staff requires to create the access system that patrons will employ is not necessarily formatted or designed for use by patrons. Understanding the requirements for various groups will better prepare the library to select or design appropriate automation systems. In preparation for a LAN, characterizing user applications for different populations will aid in granting account rights and access that protect the LAN but permit the various user groups maximum system use.

Evaluating the details of how much access various user populations require involves cooperative analysis of the functions of the library. Basically, everyone in a library has a set of tasks to perform. It is necessary for system designers and managers to understand how and why these tasks are performed in order to address the issue of satisfactory access.

Sample Initial Checklist to a Systems Analysis

1. Is there complete and comprehensive documentation for each procedure involved in handling an item? If not, this must be completed first.

2. Are the procedures being followed? If not, why not? What procedures are being followed?

3. Are there unnecessary steps or procedures? Is there a sound reason for each step, and procedure?

4. Are there flowcharts with decision statements for each procedure? If not, these should be created.

If each specialist in the various areas of library functions considers and responds to the above inquiries, it is possible to determine the appropriate level

Sample Allocation Chart

	Patrons	Staff	Administration
No. of stations	15	15	5
No. of accounts	750	40	3
Typical time on	15 min./general 45 min./research 1 hr./Internet	Circ. 10 min./contact Cat. 6 hr./day Ref. 20 min./contact Serials 6 hr./day Acq. 4 hr./day General Staff 6–8 hr./day	6–8 hr./day
Space/account	.5 MB	5 MB	5 MB
Access points	OPAC Internet	Prime biblio. db OPAC e-mail Word processors Spreadsheets Calendar Internet	LAN Admin. Prime biblio. db OPAC e-mail Word processors Spreadsheets Calendar Internet

of system rights and software access that each account, under each library activity, will require. Further, this information will provide a basis for evaluating the amount of traffic that will be handled by the system as well as provide data about how much and what kinds of equipment will be sufficient to support ongoing tasks.

Determining allocation of computing resources should be based on a clear understanding of the functions of the library, not just the technical limitations of the moment. Cost-benefit analysis of existing systems of operation compared to proposed systems should be evaluated. Just a few areas that will affect the cost of the project include network topology, number of file servers and client microcomputers, individual user account size, memory size, software requirements, number of terminals available to patrons versus the number available to the library staff, and type of monitors and keyboards. In the long run, the allocation of resources must reflect a comprehension of the role of certain tasks and services, thereby giving critical items priority in system access, or in type of computer equipment. At the same time, patrons must be satisfied with their level of access. The patron generally sees the Online Public Access Catalog (OPAC), but may have access to a variety of online bibliographic databases as well. The patron side of the LAN is facilitated via workstations or "dumb terminals" that provide limited access to the system. By necessity patrons have "read only" access to the databases. This limitation of access however should not be permitted to become an issue of concern for the patron. The interface should be comfortable and easy for the patron to use, even if making it so means managing the LAN, or performing other library tasks is more difficult. In the library, the ultimate end user is neither the library LAN managers nor the librarians but rather the patrons. Though most patrons use the computers for only short periods, it is a time when impressions about the library and library services are formed. Therefore, the quality and ease of use of those computers should be of paramount importance. At the same time, because staff will be spending significant time working at computer stations, these too need to be designed well. Just as the OPAC interface should be easy to use and visually appealing to the patron, the interface that the staff confronts should be reasonably easy to manipulate with appropriate training. All the components of the system, whether used by patron or staff should be designed to satisfy the user's needs rather than the system manager's convenience. Solid planning and attention to detail can make this a much easier task.

Documentation

Information management in a LAN is not merely the technical monitoring and control of the electronic devices and interfaces. LANs are more than electronic devices, communications centers, and storage and retrieval entities; they are tools used by people. Studies have shown that foremost to people using information systems of any kind, is accessibility (Allen and Gerstberger 1987; Culnan 1984; Rouse and Rouse 1984). LAN accessibility is dependent upon many technical factors such as the reliability of batch files and the rights assigned and restrictions imposed upon a user account. LAN accessibility is also reliant upon peoples' ability to navigate the system. Lack of adequate documentation, both technical and assistance documents, can impede the user. Research has reasonably established that people seek and use resources that are readily accessible. Access to a LAN can be daunting without documentation or training. Failure to provide adequate documentation could be construed as "gatekeeping" or attempting to protect the system or the system's information resources by excluding those who might require documentation (Markus and Bjorn-Anderson 1986; Neill 1989; Wilkin 1977).

Lack of documentation prevents LAN managers and librarians from being able to handle system failures, user errors, and upgrades in a timely fashion. System documentation representing not just technical documents but all the aspects of the system should be created and maintained. This includes documenting such aspects as the linkages from controlling batch files, software locations, user access rights, mapping patterns, drive and directory allocations, classification, and structural schemes. Record keeping to sustain system support and ensure maximum user support is critical to provision of service. Keeping the machines operating with the least disruption to the users is not simply a matter of keeping everything plugged into a power source. LANs are a matrix of interrelating devices, software interfaces, and user interaction. This makes LANs vulnerable to technical, electronic, and user error. Tracing failures requires keeping information about all possible sources of error.

Documenting the LAN is one step toward improving LAN performance. Resources must be organized in a fashion that accommodates the users; therefore, the system design would reflect the LAN's user organization. The application of directory conventions, that is, agreeing that certain types of documents reside in specified directories that are accessible to specified members, would permit the creation of work groups that have mutual access to joint work or documents that require sharing. Additionally, it would be advantageous to have file-name conventions, or agreements to how files will be labeled, dated, and identified by the users. None of these would be possible without documentation of the system structure. Hence, the breadth and scope of the server's directory system can be exploited as an organizational component to improve access while decreasing duplication, space waste, and lost documents.

Access to software applications should be documented for new users and even established users. Software groups update their product, frequently requiring that users modify how they interact with the software. In general, documentation produced by software companies is still not adequate for the average user. LAN service can be seriously damaged by users failing to comply with software instructions and requirements. Hence, LAN administration tends to bear the responsibility for creating and maintaining appropriate user-oriented documents. Further, LAN management may be the only group cognizant of unique twists in the LAN related to specific software.

Every detail of operational procedures should be documented and periodically reviewed. By having clearly defined and documented procedures for everything—from how to file the paperwork in order to add a patron to the patron base, to the steps for restarting the system after a failure—the library is ensuring the safety and efficiency of its operations. Most difficult in preparing these types of documents is including adequate detail to prevent confusion. Any procedure documents should be reviewed frequently, in fact these should be treated as "living" documents. Over time, procedures will change in response to improvements or modifications to the system.

Sample Information That Should Be Maintained About the LAN and User Accounts

• batch files: names, locations, connections to other files, last update

• rights assigned, restrictions, time limits, space allocations to accounts (system software can keep track of these)

• upgrade records for all software, repair records, error reports

• records and conventions for the location and access of software

• records and conventions for the mappings of the server and individual accounts

• records and conventions for drive and directory allocations

• conventions for filenaming

• documentation kept current about how to access specific software, how to restart if there is a failure, how to add or delete users, how to perform backups, how to report errors—all procedures relevant to each user group and written oriented to each user group.

These are but samples of the type of information that should be kept about any LAN and its users. It is essential that these records be kept current and available. A LAN becomes a complex hybrid of all the users and administrators; without conventions and documentation, it can easily become a Hydra with too many heads to cut off to control. Documentation at all levels—of the organizational structures, of the linkages between critical points—will ease the management of the system. Beginning and maintaining the documentation becomes a significant task, but one that will be seriously regretted if neglected. A number of worthwhile software packages exist to assist in the management and documentation of LANs. However, one should not overlook the external documentation requirements of patrons and staff; simple how-to documents for users about each software and interface are essential.

Documenting Structures

Documentation and procedures are critical in coping with some of the limitations of the system. It is particularly important that the software structures that control LAN functions are fully documented, such as the batch files, drivers, and system mappings.

• Batch files perform series of commands. By using a single batch file name, a batch file can, for example, change drives or directories, run software packages, or load network drivers. Batch files are meant to automate processes users may need, and thus decrease the number of key strokes users must input. Batch files also allow for modifications to be made to the system in an automated fashion in response to changes in software or in adjunct systems. Batch files exist on the computer server and on workstations; batch files may exist in any directory, local or remote, and may be executed by other batch files (Novell 1991a, 1991b).

Documenting what is in a system, as well as where it is and why it exists, is critical to managing any resource. Identification and documentation of the batch files in the system should be considered standard and required of whomever is in charge of the system. Naming conventions should be created and followed throughout the system to assist in preventing file duplication, conflict, and overlap. Records that identify all the links between batch files should be maintained. Files that automate processes and control interfaces must be documented. Lack of documentation for batch files probably contributes the most to duplication of files and failure to remove older versions of batch files.

A directory of commonly shared batch files should be constructed. Batch files that are shared via the server do not generally need to exist on workstations or in individual accounts. Organizing files that many users may need into shared directories, while complying with appropriate server and software protocols, also saves computer time, access time, and server space.

However, complex webs of batch files that connect to other batch files for no purpose other than to link two files via many other names serves no purpose. In fact, having a patchwork of batch files that may conflict with each other if started can cause unnecessary problems for tracing system failures. In addition, there are unnecessary dangers to removing batch files when many files have been overlaid on other batch files via complex webs that make it impossible to trace all the connections successfully.

Therefore, as duplicate, erroneous, or outdated batch files are found, they should be removed. While prior versions of network driver files are often retained for a period of time in case of special needs, these do not belong in active use sites in the system. Appropriate documentation must be maintained. If all the links are not identified, it could endanger the operation of the system, generate erratic system failure, or lock users out. It could be necessary to rebuild completely a server structure in order to repair this type of problem.

• Drivers are protocol programs that are created by software manufacturers and communication systems to enable computers to successfully transmit instructions and signals to printers, to terminal screens, to server computers, and so on (Novell 1991a, 1991b).

The driver designs are sometimes overridden by poorly written batch files, modified inadvertently or purposely. Without documentation, it becomes difficult to determine how the changes came about. Any modification to protocol and driver programs should be fully documented for future reference and error tracking. Any design modifications that appear ''spontaneously'' should be reported to the vendors.

• Mapping allows the user to access files that are not in the directory in which the user is working. Mapping establishes pathways that the system can access for searching without having to leave a specific location to access those other locations. Mapping identifies the drives A:, C:, H:, and so on, as well as locations in volumes or directories. Mapping is critical to efficient operation and ease of movement within the system (Novell 1991a, 1991b).

Mapping should be minimized to allow for the minimal access that a user needs. If a server's entire memory structure is mapped, that is, if every possible location is set into the standard user's map, this results in overmapping, or faulty mapping, and it will negatively affect access time. This type of mapping is not necessary for every user either, since not every user needs or has actual access to all memory locations. Faulty mapping causes the system to examine far more locations for items than necessary and may decrease access time, or even increase the potential for inappropriate accesses. Mapping a user to locations where the user does not have rights, or does not need access, may cause negative consequences, such as opening the door for security breaches or damage to executable files. Documentation of the standard mapping and any variations for individual users should be created and maintained.

CONCLUSION

This minimalistic view of LAN management requires that: a complete systems analysis be undertaken; all aspects of the system be documented and supported by documentation; an awareness of system limitations be understood; and attention be given to the user populations. The structures of LANs may be modified to a great extent, which influences how the systems function. As these systems are modified to fit particular design concerns, documentation must be maintained. In order to provide adequate access and service to the various user groups, at least the above management issues must be handled.

REFERENCES

Allen, Thomas J., and Peter Gerstberger. 1987. *Criteria for Selection of an Information Source.* Cambridge. Massachusetts Institute of Technology

Barnhart, Steve P. 1992. "The Human Angle of Network Management." *Data Com munications* 21(10) (July): 138.

Culnan, M.J. 1984. "The Dimensions of Accessibility to OnLine Information: Implications for Implementing Office Information Systems." *ACM Transactions on Office Information Systems* 2(2): 141–150.

Dauber, Steven M. 1991. "Finding Fault." *BYTE* 16(3) (March): 207–214.

Helm, Steve. 1994. "Public Access to the Internet: The Blacksburg Experience." *Virginian Librarian* 40(4) (October).

Lancaster, F. Wilfred. 1979. *Information Retrieval Systems: Characteristics, Testing and Evaluation,* 2nd ed. New York: Wiley.

Madron, T.W. 1994. *Local Area Networks: New Technologies, Emerging Standards,* 3rd ed. New York: John Wiley & Son.

Markus, M.L., and N. Bjorn-Anderson. 1986. "Power over Users: Its Exercise by Systems Professionals." Proceedings of the Seventh International Conference on Information Systems (December 15–17), pp. 224–226.

McClure, Charles R., Ann P. Bishop, Philip Doty, and Howard Rosenbaum. 1991. "Impact of Networks on Research: Results from an Empirical Study." In *The National Research and Education Network (NREN): Research and Policy Perspectives.* Norwood, N.J.: Ablex Publishing Corporation.

McKenzie, Jamieson. 1995. "Planning a Voyage into Cyberspace." *Technology Connection* 2(2) (April).

Neill, S.D. 1989. "The Information Analyst As a Quality Filter in the Scientific Communication Process." *Journal of Information Science* 15: 3–12.

Novell. 1991a. *Netware v3.11 User Basics.* Provo, Utah: Novell, Inc.

Novell. 1991b. *Netware v3.11 Concepts.* Provo, Utah: Novell, Inc.

Rouse, William B., and Sandra H. Rouse. 1984. "Human Information Seeking and Design of Information Systems." *Information Processing and Management* 20(1–2): 129–138.

Ryan, Bob, ed. 1991. "State of the Art: Network Management." *BYTE* 16(3) (March): 155–218.

Sloman, Jeffrey. 1991. "Control Central." *BYTE* 16(3) (March): 175–180.

Udell, Jon. 1991. "Networks: Trends in Network Management." *BYTE Special Issue: Outlook '92* 16(11) (November): 208–218.

Wilkin, Anne. 1977. "Personal Roles and Barriers in Information Transfer." *Advances in Librarianship* 7: 257–297.

Woodsworth, Anne. 1991. *Patterns and Options for Managing Information Technology on Campus.* Chicago: American Library Association.

3

The Evolution and Effects of a CD-ROM Network in an Undergraduate Library

Terrence F. Mech, Judith Tierney, and Jennifer L. Walz

Although CD-ROMs on stand-alone workstations were introduced to libraries in the middle to late 1980s, CD-ROM networks were not widely used in libraries prior to 1989 (Gunning, Myers, & Bailey 1993: 50). At that time, only a handful of larger institutions and those universities with engineering programs or sophisticated computer expertise operated CD-ROM networks. Today, CD-ROM networks are no longer restricted to these types of institutions. Among libraries at smaller institutions, CD-ROM networks are still found less frequently because of funding problems and lack of staff expertise.

The purpose of this chapter is to review the evolution of a CD-ROM network in an undergraduate library—ours—at a college with limited financial and personnel resources, and examine the impact of the network's development on the library's collection, personnel, and services. We will enumerate the factors that went into the decisions and experiences surrounding the evolution of our library's network. A list of helpful titles is appended.

THE NETWORK AND ITS DEVELOPMENT

King's College is a small (1,982 students) undergraduate institution awarding more than half of its baccalaureate degrees in occupational or professional disciplines. The library, containing some 150,000 volumes, is staffed by five librarians and nine support personnel. Three of the five librarians provide reference and instructional services in addition to other duties. Like many smaller colleges in the mid-1980s, there was no clear campuswide computing standard or single plan for introducing new technology. However, the launching of the library's CD-ROM network helped to break up this technological inertia.

In 1992 the library installed a small Token-ring CD-ROM network consisting of three public workstations. The Novell/CD-NET network provided individuals with access to six H.W. Wilson indexes. The network was expanded in fall 1993 to seven workstations with access to seven databases including the *National Newspaper Index*. By fall 1994 the network contained ten public workstations with additional access to the databases available through the campus network. The CD-ROM network also serves as the center of a buildingwide network that provides librarians and staff with connections to the campus network and the Internet. As you will see, this network project did not emerge all at once but rather evolved in stages.

In 1987 the library installed its first CD-ROM database (a Wilson index) on a single IBM personal computer. It was intended to facilitate students' use of the journal collection. By 1990 the library had four Wilson CD-ROM indexes on two stand-alone workstations. Since each station contained only two databases and could only support one user, only two people could search simultaneously. The two users were limited to the two databases on their respective stations. Individuals wanting to search a different database had to change workstations. Concerned with the growing number of students who had to wait to use particular indexes, the librarians decided to develop a local area network (LAN) within the library. We had two goals at this point: to make each database searchable from any workstation, and to mechanize the changing of CD-ROM discs.

Tape-loading databases on the public catalog was considered but rejected. The software to do this was still in its early stages and the library did not want to be a test site. In addition, there was not enough room on the library's integrated system (Dynix) for the databases, nor were there funds to upgrade or replace the system.

Although the library had installed an integrated library system in 1989, personal-computer expertise among the librarians was limited and networking experience was nonexistent. A recently hired reference librarian with some formal computer training was appointed to serve as the network coordinator. While some previous computer experience is necessary, most network managers are self-taught and ours was no exception. The curriculum included a large amount of reading (manuals and computer magazines—*PC Magazine, PC Computing, PC World, Computing World, BYTE, Information Today, Information Technology & Libraries, Netware Technical Journal, LAN Times,* and *CD-ROM Professional*) and practice (playing around with the software).

In preparation for the network, the librarians met with computing center personnel to review how networks function. After a discussion of the plans for a campus-wide network, the merits of remaining compatible with the computing center were obvious. This was reinforced by observations of the support problems other departments experienced when they made equipment and software choices at variance with the computing center's expertise. Remaining uniform (hardware and software) with the computing center would eliminate needless complications and ensure additional technical support and backup.

Networking CD-ROMs is constrained by the triangle principle. Three basic elements in the design and operation of a perfect LAN are: speed, low expense, and ease of operation. However, with the current technology it is only possible to have two of the three corners of the triangle. The most likely combinations are to have a network that is cheap and simple, but slow; or to have an expensive network that is fast and easy to operate and use.

After site visits to two larger libraries with networks, the serious examination of the networking options began. We decided to implement a fast but easy to operate and use network, building it in stages as funds permitted. Based on our observations of database and online catalog users, we knew response time would be important. We also wanted an expandable network that would be easy for the staff to maintain and would be easy for students and faculty to use.

The criterion for hardware was that it be compatible with the computing center and its network. In reality this criterion translated into the same hardware standard as the computing center—IBM equipment, Token-ring network typology, and Novell network software. Although less expensive equipment could have been purchased, the potential problems of compatibility, support, and service were considered unacceptable long-term risks—in terms of the financial and human costs. We decided that it would be easier and less expensive to purchase familiar brand-name equipment from well-established vendors that our campus computer staff preferred than it would be to obtain additional personnel to troubleshoot a network built with less expensive equipment from newer firms. In the event of trouble, the equipment's uniformity and compatibility would reduce the number of potential complications and the likelihood of finger-pointing by vendors.

With the hardware platform determined, we wanted a software-only solution that would be mounted on off-the-shelf computer equipment, rather than a vendor's prepackaged, turnkey, CD-ROM network composed of proprietary hardware and software. Although this decision eliminated a number of possible turnkey alternatives, it also reduced the possibility that the network would be artifically dependent on or restricted by a vendor's limitations. Although a turnkey system with its single source for equipment and support is theoretically easier to purchase and maintain, you do pay a premium for the convenience.

Once we had chosen Novell network operating system software, we started to select the software required to connect and operate the CD-ROMs over the network. Our criteria for CD-ROM–networking software was that it be relatively simple, flexible, fast, reliable, and able to operate in an IBM and Novell environment. There were two basic CD-networking choices, with several software options: peer-to-peer (Lantastic) or client-server (CD-NET, Opti-Net, SCSI Express). The peer-to-peer method had the qualities of being cheap and easy. However, it was slow, not too secure, and frequently unreliable. Since our criteria were fast and easy, our only other choice was the client-server method. Fortunately there were a number of good software programs.

A review of the trade literature (Betts, Pastrick, & Perratore 1991; Thompson & Maxwell 1990) revealed three solid contenders: CD-NET, SCSI Express, and Opti-Net. At the time SCSI Express was rated the fastest, but it had problems with CDs that required the use of Microsoft's CD-ROM Extensions (MSCDEX). Since we were not sure which CD-ROM databases we might be networking in the future, this was a potential problem. CD-NET and Opti-Net were each examined against our criteria of fast and easy. Although both products met the criteria, CD-NET offered a Network Loadable Module (NLM) version (which would work tightly with Novell) and a built-in menu interface. In addition CD-NET was faster than Opti-Net and had been chosen by *PC Magazine* as an Editor's Choice (Betts, Pastrick, & Perratore 1991).

In addition to the published sources, an Internet discussion group (CDROM-LAN, "Use of CDROM Products in LAN Environments" <CDROM-LAN@idbsu. idbsu.edu>) proved to be a great source of practical information and useful advice from networking veterans. CDROMLAN is dedicated to the use of CD-ROM products in LAN environments and to the problems of networking various products. The list is owned and moderated by Dan Lester, Network Information Coordinator, Boise State University Library, Boise, Idaho.

Vendors and their support services were frequent sources of information. The information they supplied and the questions they asked us served as a type of "reality check" on our proposed plans.

In planning the network the decision was made to take a multiyear view and design a multipurpose, buildingwide network rather than just a ten station CD-ROM public network for reference. This would provide flexibility for future growth within the building and facilitate the development of a campus network without having to redevelop sections of the installed network. The idea was also in our minds that the library's existing integrated system would eventually be replaced by an automated system that was designed to take advantage of network technology. The decision to remain uniform with the computing center and to build a fast and relatively easy to use and operate network meant that the network would be expensive and would have to be built in sections as funds permitted.

Building the network in stages proved to be a good financial, learning, and human resources strategy. Besides being easier to budget for, it made the project much more manageable and helped to reduce the risks involved. With the network coordinator in the lead, existing personnel were used to research, design, and install the network. Individuals gained a better understanding of networking than they would have gotten with a turnkey system. With our own personnel involved, the project seemed less of a technological threat or wonder. Because we didn't bring in outside help, the measured growth also kept the project humanly possible for existing staff. The controlled installation provided time for learning, permitted the exploration of options, and allowed us to take in stride the surprises that came from unexamined assumptions.

Although the network cable had been pulled during the winter by personnel from the college's physical plant and the equipment and software ordered in the late spring, nothing arrived in the sequence expected or needed. After all the equipment arrived and some initial learning experiences with the CD-ROM drives and the Novell software, the network was fully operational within six working days. With just three days before fall classes began, the librarians and staff were introduced to the network.

In thinking about the network and what to put on it, we decided early in the planning stages to stay with and expand the selection of H.W. Wilson databases currently offered for a variety of reasons: we were already familiar with the company and the product; the databases were easy for undergraduates to search and students were comfortable with the software interface; the databases were relatively simple to explain or demonstrate; the uniformity of the interface made it easy for students to move from one index to another; and the indexes provided access to a large number of the journals held by the library. Wilson's commitment to provide abstracts was an added attraction. As a company, H.W. Wilson was responsive to our needs and the licensing arrangements were very reasonable. The various configuration options also were comprehensive and flexible. Our subsequent experience with other database vendors has reaffirmed our original choice.

A primary consideration for adding items to the network was the database's ability to return users to the network menu. Once users had their information, they frequently just walked away, rather than exiting from the program. This meant that anyone wanting to use that station had to figure out what index they were in, determine where they were in the program, exit it, and return to the main menu before they could start their search. With a campus network this would mean that ports could be needlessly tied up, if users did not correctly exit the database. Software without a time-out feature, which automatically returns to a DOS prompt (network menu) after a period of inactivity, was deemed unacceptable. Although some people said that undergraduates should be able to figure these things out, we felt differently. Ideally individuals should be able to do these things; however, based on our experience, the fewer obstacles users of all ages have to deal with, the better. An individual's lack of computer or software expertise should not be a handicap to using this network. Several databases that are ''technically networkable'' are not networkable in our definition.

We realized that the cost and licensing agreements of some desirable databases would probably keep them off our network for a while. There were also some databases that would have been nice to have but were not necessary in an undergraduate environment. ''Networkable'' also does not mean it should be on a network.

MAINTENANCE

There have been no major problems with the network. On occasion the token-ring cable connections worked loose, just enough to cause a workstation to lock up. Now the connections are kept out of harm's way and checked regularly. The other problem we encountered was due to a power outage. A campus-wide electrical outage tripped a fuse in the CD-ROM–drive tower. We did not discover the tower fans were not working until three weeks later, when the CD-ROM drives started to overheat and malfunction. Reinserting the fuses restarted the fans.

Initially, the network used the same makes and models of computing equipment; unfortunately, it did not stay that way for long. Our printers were the first to break this uniformity.

Because of the openness of the reference area (thus the need for quiet printing), we relied on our previous experience and chose Hewlett Packard Think-Jet printers when we built the network. However, the cartridges for ink-jet printers were expensive. The cost was considered a trade-off because they were easy to use and care for. Unfortunately, sometimes good products are discontinued by manufacturers. When it came time to expand the network, a good replacement printer was not readily apparent.

Four new printers were ordered sight unseen on the basis of their technology and word-of-mouth recommendations. This was a mistake. The new dot-matrix printers were as quiet as expected, but not as quiet as the ink-jet printers. But the real problem was the paper feed, which tended to jam frequently and was difficult to clear. We should have tested a machine before we purchased four printers.

In the end, the greatest source of network aggravation for the reference librarians were and are the printers and their maintenance. Although efforts are made to check the cartridges or ribbons and stock them with paper, the printers inevitably "run out" when reference activity is busiest.

Although the network has been relatively trouble-free, the amount of time required for system-related maintenance has been more than expected. Keeping the network at peak performance is facilitated by regular hardware and software maintenance. The intent is to prevent problems before they develop. On a regular basis the printers are inspected (ink, print-heads, sprockets, oil gears, etc.). Dust is a problem, so filters on the CD-ROM drives and the CD-ROM lenses are cleaned once a semester. Keeping the dust off the monitors and out of keyboards keeps them attractive and functional. The inside of the server and workstations are vacuumed whenever they are opened up.

In addition to hardware maintenance, software upkeep is important. Network error files are checked and the DOS "CHKDSK" procedure is run regularly on the workstations. The "CHKDSK" command (a disk-checking utility) analyzes the directories, files, and file allocation table on the disk; it produces a disk and memory status report. The network traffic, cache buffers, packets, and memory are monitored frequently for signs of trouble. Status reports on the network's "health" are run regularly.

The TRACE.LOG file on the WilsonDisc program keeps track of the commands, the search terms, and the databases used during search sessions. These TRACE.LOG files provide statistics and a profile of database use. This information not only tells us which Wilson databases are being used, but how often and in what ways. The statistics make it possible to track growth and changes in network activity and searching behavior from year to year.

Upgrades and enhancements in hardware and software frequently contain some kind of surprise or new learning experience. We have found that some software that works before a new release does not always work after a new release. In the process it becomes apparent that assumptions about what is required or how something works cannot be made based on previous experience. Likewise, it is not uncommon for a database update to contain an intermittent "problem," which locks up a workstation or two. In such cases, it takes a while to determine if the problem is network- or software-related. When the vendors are contacted, they frequently are aware of the problem and are willing to mail out a replacement disc.

According to Timothy Dugdale, a reference librarian/computer specialist at Georgia State University, LAN maintenance varies according to several factors: (1) the number of individuals who are able to assist with it; (2) the reliability and stability of your system and equipment, particularly the amount of memory available; and (3) the number of other functions, such as word processing or electronic mail (e-mail), that also run on the CD-ROM network. A related factor is the number of personnel who can train or assist individuals in the use of the network. Dugdale reports that in his situation, with a split position between reference and the network, 70 percent of his time is devoted to computers (Internet correspondence, July 13, 1993). Time is also taken up by training staff, and apprising them of software updates and changes in the setup. The size of the network and the degree of hardware and software standardization also influence how much time is devoted to LAN maintenance.

In our situation, one reference librarian splits her time between the network and reference, with initially 60 to 70 percent of her time devoted to network-related maintenance or troubleshooting. The actual time that can be devoted to the network is limited to about three hours each afternoon. This librarian is scheduled to work four hours at the reference desk each evening. Currently, no other personnel are trained to assist with the network. Since the network is fairly stable, only a small amount of time is devoted to dealing with problems per se. The largest amount of time is spent dealing with upgrades, software changes, and anomalies in upgrades.

Communication among library personnel is important. Conveying information about network-related changes is an integral part of network administration. This is particularly true if the changes may affect users. Because of its complexities, it is critical to document the state of the network. It is important to keep the manuals, documentation, and information about the hardware configuration and software in a central and easily accessible location. Knowing the details and keeping track of them for emergencies is vital but easily overlooked.

At the present time we are developing more complete documentation. In addition to the configuration information and the telephone numbers of the various technical support personnel, the documentation contains descriptions of likely problems and the steps necessary to diagnose and correct them. In writing the documentation we are trying to anticipate the assumptions of personnel more familiar with networking, such as those who have a working knowledge of DOS. Two manuals are being developed: a procedures manual for the network coordinator (with corollary Netware materials) and a troubleshooting/emergency manual for use by others, when the network coordinator is not available.

Cooperation with the computing center provides us with backup only. We consider the network a critical operation, because if it is down it causes public service problems. Though we have a good relationship with the computing center and they are willing to help, they are often too busy to deal with our problems right away. They are also not familiar with CD-ROM networks. For these reasons it is important to have good documentation and to keep problems in check. Currently, if the network coordinator is unavailable to deal with network problems, there is some difficulty in solving them in a timely manner.

We have not yet discarded most of our print indexes in favor of the CD-ROM medium. Even if we have no network, students will still have access to the information; it just will not be as easy to access as they are accustomed. However, financial considerations and practicality may dictate that we reduce this duplication.

RESULT AND OBSERVATIONS

When looking at a technological advancement like a CD-ROM network, it is easy to lose sight of the fact that it is only a tool to facilitate the use of information and remove impediments for those who use libraries and their resources. As a tool it really does not have a life all of its own, only the life we give it. Like any success there is a tendency to build on it, figuring that more of a good thing is better. This is not always so, at least not right away. The ramifications and implications sometime need to be digested and the lessons studied before proceeding further.

JOURNAL USE AND RAMIFICATIONS

Previously, students were reluctant to use journals, preferring to find what they needed in books rather than consult paper indexes. With the introduction of journal indexes on CD-ROM, students are more willing to use newspapers and journals and, with the network, are regularly searching multiple indexes. However, students remain reluctant to go back to older print indexes when necessary. Students' use of the networked indexes has greatly reduced the number of paper indexes to be reshelved.

While use of the CD-ROMs has reduced the number of index volumes to be reshelved, it has greatly increased the number of journal and newspaper items (print and microfilm) to be reshelved. Use of the newspaper and journal collections has increased an estimated 379 percent between 1983 and 1992. In 1983 an average of 420 items (issues/volumes/reels of microfilm) were reshelved per week. By 1991 the influence of the CD-ROM indexes on stand-alone stations was evident; an average of 1,562 items per week were reshelved. Upon implementation of the network, journal use increased again. In 1992 an average of 2,011 items per week were reshelved, a 28.7 percent increase over 1991.

Along with the increase in the number of items reshelved, there was a 35 percent increase in the number of titles used. In 1991, 386 titles were used at least once. In 1992, 524 titles were used at least once. While more titles were being used, some of the most heavily used titles in 1983 were still among the most used in 1991 and 1992. The top 25 titles, 5 percent of the titles, accounted for 56 percent of the use in 1992.

While the list of the most heavily used titles has not changed dramatically, the volume of activity has changed. The descent from the heaviest to the least used title was more gradual and less precipitous in 1992 than it was in 1991. Just as there was stability at the top, there was also stability at the bottom of the list. The number of seldom used titles did not vary much—12 percent in 1991 and 11 percent in 1992.

The addition of a single database to the network can have a dramatic influence on journal use. The library has subscribed to *General Science Index* in paper since 1983 but did not install it on the network until 1992. Networking *General Science Index* resulted in a 22 percent rise in the number of science titles used and significantly more use of those titles that had been previously utilized.

To more accurately gauge the increase in journal use, interlibrary loan activity must also be considered. While faculty interlibrary loans for journal articles remained relatively stable, only 6.8 percent growth, student interlibrary loans for journal articles increased 86 percent in 1992 compared with 1991.

Although the computerized indexes allow students to search several years of journal articles, it is frustrating to users who equate access with ownership. With the rise in journal use came complaints about the number of journals in the library. The contrast—between the satisfaction of having quick access to the journal citations and the frustration of not having similar access to all the articles found—is unsettling for both students and faculty. Other libraries with CD-ROM indexes report similar phenomena, increased journal use along with complaints about the number of journal titles available.

Heightened expectations as to what technology will do for them during the research process may also contribute to unrealistic expectations. Many individuals equate improved technological access with instant physical possession of the article. Technology makes their work easier, but it does not eliminate the most important work involved in the research process: the interaction of researchers and their materials.

IMPACT ON STUDENT RESEARCH

The introduction of stand-alone, CD-ROM indexes in the library had a dramatic qualitative and quantitative impact on the way students researched. Moving from the stand-alone station to a network had a further dramatic quantitative impact. Because of the easy access CD-ROM indexes provide to periodicals and newspaper articles, students were far more likely to see them as viable sources of information. Before CDs, students might have been willing to check a volume or two of a printed index. They were far more interested in finding a book on their subject. With CDs, the students checked several years of one or more indexes more quickly and easily than they could have checked two years of the print sources. As a result, students were finding their way to substantial numbers of journal and newspaper articles. Just as the automation of the catalog produced increased book use, computerization of the indexes produced increased periodical use.

This transformation is not only the result of ease of access and use, real and significant as it is, but also because of the ''glamour'' of using a computerized database rather than the old-fashioned print database. In addition, faculty, conscious of the mandate to develop the computer and information skills of students, give research assignments that encourage and specifically require students to use certain CD-ROM databases, thereby accomplishing several pedagogical goals simultaneously. However, faculty and librarians express frustration at students' reluctance to search print sources when computerized versions are not available or not appropriate. The ''learned helplessness'' and lack of intellectual initiative of some students may be at least partially explained by the presence of the computer.

The network permits users to move from one database to another without physically relocating, thus allowing them to quickly and easily massage relevant materials from several sources, and giving them much larger quantities of citations than the previous stand-alone stations. A problem is that many students tend to confuse quantity with quality. Thus, it becomes even more important for individuals to have the intellectual tools necessary to analyze information sources. Doing research has become simultaneously easier and more complicated. It promises to become more so in the foreseeable future, and we have to find ways to address this issue. Students use the research strategies they believe will give them the greatest benefits with the least cost in time or effort, and electronic resources are perceived as the most effective way of accomplishing this objective (Valentine 1993: 300–304).

When students used printed indexes, the time and effort needed to read and write the citations acted as an automatic filtering system. Students evaluated and selected citations using their own criteria as they read them and before they wrote them down. That physical filtering system is no longer operational in the network environment.

In some respects the network makes it easier for students to work together or ask for assistance. When a computer is involved, some students find it easier to ask for assistance from those around them, just like they do in the computer labs. It is not uncommon to find students huddled over a computer discussing the contents of a screen display and then returning to their separate computers. A concern of the reference librarians is the accuracy of either the information or the strategies that students are sharing with each other. Students teaching each other ineffective strategies or passing on bad information is not in anyone's best interest.

IMPACT ON REFERENCE PERSONNEL

In a satisfaction survey, first-year students report that the CD-ROM databases are their favorite service, with reference services ranked fourth. By students' junior and senior years, the CD-ROM databases have slipped to second place with references services ranked first. It appears that undergraduates at first gravitate toward machines and technology; but as they progress with their education, they come to appreciate the librarians' expertise.

How should reference and other service points be staffed in the CD-ROM–network environment? There are two levels of need for undergraduates using CD-ROM technology: (1) the need for technical expertise to physically access the data. This is fairly simple and straight-forward compared to (2) the need for information skills to intellectually access the information. This is far more complicated and profound.

The first need merely requires some instruction and experience in manipulating the hardware and software. Although a great deal of time may be needed, it can be accomplished rather easily—either individually or in groups—by support staff with basic credentials. (This could be considered a training need. This same support staff could be responsible for the daily care of the network, such as keeping paper in the printers, changing ribbons or cartridges, eliminating paper jams.)

The second need of achieving intellectual access to the data is an educational need. Students need to learn how to think, understand how the database is constructed, and understand how the literature is structured in the discipline. While this also can be achieved in individual or group settings, it requires a higher level of expertise and credentials on the part of the instructor. The acquisition of these skills and knowledge is cumulative, subtle, and crucial.

Although this need has always been there, it is writ large when students are working with computerized databases—probably because of the software's accounting functions. The ability to store and print the kinds of searches students do tells us directly what we could only suspect when students were using print sources—that their ability to think is critical to their ability to research effectively. Networking the stand-alone CD-ROM databases provides a "multiplier" effect: it magnifies the impact of this realization.

We know now that when students use terms such as "education" to search *ERIC* or "business" to search *Wilson Business Abstracts,* they are not approaching the databases intelligently. A surprising number of students start out using "big" words (e.g., education) to search specific topics (e.g., dropouts). However, when students are struck by the sheer volume or the total lack of citations, they frequently generate a series of reference questions to narrow their searches. Although students may be quite content with their CD-ROM searches, an examination of their strategies indicates a real need for more and better computer research instruction (Brady, Nolan, & Whitmore 1993).

Although a connection exists between the technical manipulation of the database and the intellectual access of the data, the distinction between these two levels of learning may require us to take a radical new look at both the kind of staff needed to best serve the needs of students in an undergraduate environment and the kind of instruction needed. We really need a library classroom for teaching. The lack of a networked instructional facility limits the type and effectiveness of the network training and instruction the librarians can provide. A training facility with hands-on capabilities would help librarians to teach students the most effective ways to utilize the databases and the network. Point-of-use instruction, in any form, only goes so far.

DISCUSSION

From an administrative standpoint, the creation of the network was a project the library did not want to avoid. The library is trying to shape its future rather than have it shaped by others. The situation on campus was such that the library's network sparked the computing center's interest, and spurred the discussion and development of other network-related projects on campus. As a result, the library's CD-ROM network provided something to put on the fledgling campus network. The project has fostered better understanding and good relations between the computing center and the library. As the campus network develops, these relationships have proven to be mutually beneficial. A recognition of common interests can be advanced through cooperation.

Would we do it again? Certainly, students are using more materials than they ever have. In addition to providing better service to users, it is a great form of staff development and self-study. At times the project does strain personnel and financial resources. We are learning to pace ourselves. There is less of a "necessity" to do it all at once. The project forces the library to examine the way it does business. The need to address how we will meet the growing needs of our users is never far from our minds. We now spend more time trying to anticipate the effects of proposed changes. In looking at what needs to be accomplished to implement a more technologically advanced library, it is easy to forget just how much progress has been made. It is important to remember that while there are libraries further ahead or behind technologically, we need to focus on answering the question: Are we doing our best to meet the information needs of our users?

REFERENCES

Betts, Kellyn, Greg Pastrick, and Ed Perratore, 1991. "Networking CD-ROMs: The Power of Shared Access." *PC Magazine* 10(19): 333–363.

Brady, Fern E., Anne C. Nolan, and Marilyn P. Whitmore. 1993. "Networking CD-ROMs: An Evaluation with Implications for Improving Service." *Journal of Academic Librarianship* 19(3): 140–143.

Gunning, Kathleen, Judy E. Myers, and Charles W. Bailey. 1993. "Networked Electronic Information Systems at the University of Houston Libraries: The IRIS Project and Beyond." *Library Hi Tech* 11(4): 49–55, 83.

Thompson, M. Keith, and Kimberly Maxwell. 1990. "Networking CD-ROMs." *PC Magazine* 9(14): 237–260.

Valentine, Barbara. 1993. "Undergraduate Research Behavior: Using Focus Groups to Generate Theory." *Journal of Academic Librarianship* 19(5): 300–304.

SELECTED BIBLIOGRAPHY

Abella, Gilbert V., and Paul W. Kittle. 1992. "The CD-ROM Experience at Loma Linda: The Issues of Training, Logistics, and Creative Financing." *Medical Reference Services* 11 (Summer): 1–11.

Atkinson, Roderick D., and John R. Yokley. 1993. "Multiplatform CD-ROM Networking." *CD-ROM Professional* 6 (May): 73–78, 81.

Bard, Nancy. 1993. "Networking CD-ROMs: A Case Study." *Journal of Youth Services in Libraries* 6(2): 185–189.

Breeding, Marshall, ed. 1992. *Library LANs: Case Studies in Practice & Application.* Westport, Conn.: Meckler.

Burnett, Jim, and G. Merguerian. 1992. "Networking CD-ROMs at the Seton Hall University Library." *New Jersey Libraries* 25 (Fall): 32–34.

Cain, Mark. 1993. "Simple and Inexpensive CD-ROM Networking: A Step-by-Step Approach." *Information Technology and Libraries* 12 (June): 262–266.

Chen, Ching-Chih. 1991. *Optical Discs in Libraries: Uses & Trends.* Medford, N.J.: Information, Inc.

Cummins, Thompson R., and John Shipley. 1992. "Local CD-ROM Networking: Evaluation and Planning." *Public Libraries* 31(2): 99–102.

Desmarais, Norman, ed. 1991. *CD-ROM Local Area Networks: A User's Guide.* Westport, Conn.: Meckler.

Duggan, Mary K., ed. 1990. *CD-ROM in the Library.* Boston: G.K. Hall & Co.

Grant, Marilyn A., and John C. Stalker. 1989. "The Multiplatter CD-ROM Network at Boston College." *Laserdisk Professional* 2 (September): 12–18.

Harris, Richard J. 1991. "Installation of an Opti-Net CD-ROM LAN at Eastern Virginia Medical School." *CD-ROM Professional* 4 (January): 25–26.

Hartman, Joel L., and Ellen I. Watson. 1993. "BLISS: The Bradley Library Information Support System." *Library Hi Tech* 11(3): 19–36.

James, Jonathan K. 1993. "CD-ROM in the Information Marketplace: A Comprehensive Study From UMI." *CD-ROM Professional* 6 (July): 102–105.

Kittle, Paul W. 1993. "Networking the Light Fantastic: CD-ROMs on LANs." *CD-ROM Professional* 5 (January): 30–35.

Kritz, Harry M., Nikhil Jain, and E. Alan Armstrong. 1991. "An Environmental Approach to CD-ROM Networking Using Off-the-Shelf Components." *CD-ROM Professional* 4 (July): 24–29.

Marks, Kenneth E. et al. 1993. "CD-ROM and Local Area Networks." *Computers in Libraries* 13 (April): 19–33, 52.

Marks, Kenneth E and Steven P. Neilsen. 1991. *Local Area Networks in Libraries*. Westport, Conn.: Meckler.

Nickerson, Gord. 1990. "Installing a Low-Cost CD-ROM Network." *CD-ROM End User* 2(2): 26–29.

Nissley, Meta, and Nancy M. Nelson, eds. 1990. *CD-ROM Licensing & Copyright Issues for Libraries*. Westport, Conn.: Meckler.

Paul, David, Joyce Lathan, Keith Mitchell, and John Nikirk, 1991. "The Over-the-Counter CD-ROM Network Solution." *CD-ROM Librarian* 6 (October): 19–23.

Reese, Jean. 1989. "CD-ROM Technology at Vanderbilt University: Impact on Library Staff and the Educational Community." *Optical Information Systems* (January–February): 38–43.

Thornburg, Barbara J. 1992. "CD-ROM and the Academic Reference Librarian: A Review of the Literature." *The Electronic Library* 10 (August): 219–221.

Wright, Keith. 1990. *Workstations & Local Area Networks for Libraries*. Chicago: American Library Association.

4

Managing a Campus-Wide Information Service

Tom Klingler and Rick Wiggins

The University of Akron is a heavily wired campus, having recently passed the 100-mile mark in installed fiber optic cable. In computing terms, it is also a diverse campus. At least three types of e-mail systems are well established; computing platforms are extremely varied, extending from terminal-based mainframe systems through microcomputer-based desktop systems and on to high-powered computational and graphics workstations. The library has a decade of local systems experience, and has recently installed its second generation online system as part of its move into the OhioLINK project—a project linking library catalogs and services of all public higher education institutions in the state of Ohio. In the midst of this information-rich campus, there was until recently a large unmet need for a campus-wide information service (CWIS). As the computer center addressed this need and set a goal of installing a CWIS, its network operations office first asked what the goals of such a project would be.

PROJECT GOALS

With any automation project, the first thing to do is to define the project goals. In setting up a campus-wide information service, one must first ask the question: What do we want such a service to do? The first answer sounds simple: We want it to provide certain types of information campus-wide, and indeed worldwide, on a minimal budget, with no increases in staffing, across multiple computer platforms. We want it to be easy to use and easy to maintain. We want it to be able to handle potentially huge amounts of data with minimal overhead. We want the system to be a combined effort of a lot of people across campus. If people from many offices mount and maintain information on the CWIS, then the workload is distributed; the need for new personnel is minimized.

Again, the first organizational principle for any automation project is to clearly define the project goals. This chapter has several goals: first, to describe the steps and principles involved in managing a CWIS, as illustrated by the Akron experience, and second to indicate a body of organizational principles to facilitate any automation project.

TYPES AND SOURCES OF INFORMATION

Another important consideration in defining an automation project is defining the scope of the information to be processed. If this scope is not well defined, the resulting project may not deliver the information needed by the campus. The type and amount of information to be provided will drive many of the most important management decisions; for example, what software will be used.

At The University of Akron, the CWIS task force agreed to mount all types of information: press releases, student registration and advising information, library hours, and book store information to name a few. It was decided to maintain only text-based information. This decision was based on the fact that more than 500 text-only terminals were still in use by people needing access to the CWIS. In addition, being primarily commuters, many students would be accessing the service using low-speed, dial-in connections that support only text-based information.

The decision to limit the service to text-based information was clearly a compromise between an ideal and the various hardware realities on campus. This compromise was reached only after an honest, global look at the project's hardware environment. Such an examination is an important early step in the planning process for any automation project.

User Authentication

A close look at the project's information environment is equally vital. Concerning the potential information for a CWIS project, it will often be found that some information (such as student records) cannot be released to everyone. If this type of information is to be provided, a more complex system capable of authenticating the user is required. The files necessary for authentication can increase the system's requirements for size, budget, and maintenance. Authenticating users of one system by passing them through another system on which they have an authorized account can sometimes be a solution to this problem. But such a solution can add its own layers of complexity and overhead. This problem of user authentication applies to many campus information projects, including user-initiated library loans and document requests as well as remote access to proprietary bibliographic databases and Internet services. Various methods to authenticate users are becoming generally available. The Kerberos system from Project Athena at the Massachusetts Institute of Technology allows for an individual's single password to be used for authentication on any number of cooperating information services. Kerberos passwords are encrypted before being sent across the network, adding to the security of the overall system. The use of smart-card systems allows for an additional level of security. Users must not only be in possession of a valid user account and password, but also a credit card–sized microprocessor that displays a coded sequence of numbers specific to that user's account. Even if the user account and password are discovered by someone else, they are of no use without the corresponding smart card. The planning for such an authentication system clearly must be campus-wide in scope; the technology can be used to control access to a variety of resources and services from food services to library databases.

Other questions about the type of data to be provided by an automation project also help determine the complexity of the resulting system. For example, if any of the system's information is to be provided by the user, the system will have to be interactive, hence necessarily more complex, and maybe more difficult for the users to learn. If the service is to be accessible to the general public, certain information, like proprietary bibliographic databases, may have legally restricted access; mechanisms will need to be available to accomplish this restriction Mechanisms like concurrent user metering and network address filtering can require higher maintenance, as they add complexities above and beyond the authentication technologies mentioned previously.

Departmental Contributions

Public relations departments are a natural source of organizational information, and they may consider the electronic dissemination of their information as a logical next step to the printed version. At The University of Akron, the public relations department has been actively involved in the CWIS planning from the beginning, and now their normal routine includes posting all university news releases on the CWIS.

Data that is maintained by an institutional research department can represent a great source of information for a CWIS. Many organizations depend upon such a centralized facility for organization-wide information management. Examples of such information include: personnel data for an online directory; student records and enrollment data; course descriptions, room assignments, class meeting times, and required textbooks; and calendars of campus events. Much of this data may be stored in database management systems in the central computing department, allowing information to be extracted and formatted by software programs into effective reports. Organizations that allow the campus's departmental staff direct access to data will be able to provide this information quickly for the CWIS. Those that depend upon the central computing department for such extraction, formatting, and reporting services may find that other work has higher priority and the time required to get the information into the CWIS may be painfully long.

THE LIBRARIAN MANAGER

At this early juncture in a CWIS project, defining the scope of information and determining its initial organization, the library can serve the campus well. Experienced in researching and finding information, in understanding and addressing the global information needs of its campus-wide constituency, in organizing information logically for a wide range of consumers, and in using automated systems all the while—the library staff is poised like no other to build the structure of a CWIS most successfully. Indeed, if structure and politics permit it, the CWIS manager might best be a lead librarian who is accomplished in these skills. Building a CWIS provides a good opportunity for building a partnership with the computer center. The CWIS system administrator most likely should come from the computer center. And, for the CWIS to be successful, the manager and system administrator need to have a close working relationship.

Not providing the information required by the campus is a sure ingredient for the failure of any automation project. Users of a CWIS are interested in finding specific information for specific needs. If the service does not fulfill those needs, they will stop using it. The analysis of what information people need and how that information will be obtained is as critical an aspect in establishing a CWIS as it is for any information management project.

LOCATION OF INFORMATION

Determining the information to be provided also requires consideration of where the information will reside. Less effort will be required if most of the information is centrally managed; however, this may not be the case. Many publications are not produced on campus and will require additional effort to be made available. Some organizations use off-campus printing services; student newspapers, for example, often are printed by commercial printing firms. This practice can be a source of problems since these services sometimes are not prepared to provide electronic copies of their publications. Getting electronic copies of these publications may often entail an additional cost and additional processing, like manual retyping or scanning of the publication, to prepare it for use on the CWIS.

Access versus Security

A world of information is available via the Internet. If any of this information is included, access issues will need to be considered. Matters of network security and Internet etiquette have never been more important. At The University of Akron, the computer center and the library each chose, under the portions of the CWIS that each manages, to provide access to many Internet resources. Providing access to some resources on the Internet requires the use of the re-mote-access service known as "telnet," which connects the user's machine to a remote machine linked to the Internet. When not properly controlled within the CWIS, telnet's power to establish remote connections can be abused. Such abuse can occur most easily if the system provides the user an open telnet prompt, that is, the prompt: "telnet> " waiting for the user to input a desti-nation machine address. Such an open prompt allows the user the potential to connect to any other machine on the Internet, opening an avenue for potential hackers, who are bent on compromising remote systems.

Such a situation is the network manager's nightmare, but it has a good chance of becoming a reality when a CWIS is set up—especially if access to the CWIS is provided at unsupervised public workstations in a library or computer lab. Even if the local system manager is careful to eliminate any open telnet access from the local machine, it is impossible to eliminate such access from other sites to which users may connect from the local site. Hence, a core question to be addressed in CWIS planning is this: What is the institutional stance on the continuum that ranges from open access to the Internet on the one hand, to the strictest control on the other?

ORGANIZATIONAL SUPPORT

No matter what decisions are made about the type and amount of information to be provided, no information management project will be successful without the support of the organization's administration. Getting the top academic and administrative officers to support the project is critical to its success. Lack of support from the administration can result in the absence of key information. Many organizations have information scattered across multiple departments, and often the departments that control the most important information are also the busiest. Some of these may not see the benefit of spending their limited resources to make their information available to a wider constituency that they do not necessarily recognize. In fact, some may even consider making their information more widely available as a "loss of control" issue and refuse to participate. Only a convinced administration can provide the leadership to pull all parts of the organization together to accomplish this task. Once the departments see that the administration wants this service to succeed and that its success depends on everyone's participation, it becomes much easier for them to find the necessary resources to place their information on the service. Ideally, department partici-pation in the information management project would become a documented goal in all departments' planning and evaluation processes.

Middle Management Support

The supervisors of the Information Providers (IPs), the employees in various departments throughout the campus who maintain their departmental information on the CWIS, will need to be aware of the efforts these people are making to provide a valuable resource to the organization. Too often this type of activity remains invisible to the management and, therefore, unrecognized. Making certain that the IPs' efforts are recognized will certainly motivate them to continue to participate.

Not providing sufficient support for the IPs is a sure route to failure. IPs need training, timely assistance, motivation, and rewards. Without such support, few of them will contribute effectively and promptly to the service. For most organizations, there is no CWIS without IPs. The success of a CWIS is in these people's hands. The service manager must be ready and able to provide the support they need, or face the almost inevitable failure of the service. Often this failure is not the service manager's fault, but the lack of commitment by management. Service managers who are spread too thinly will not be able to provide the necessary support. This fact applies to any sort of information management project, not just a CWIS.

SUMMARY OF GENERAL REQUIREMENTS

To this point, we have examined the general requirements for a CWIS, which are the requirements for any successful automation project. They include:

1. defining the project goals;
2. defining the scope of information to be managed, which includes an examination of the project's information environment;
3. examining the project's hardware environment;
4. examining the issues of information access and licensing, system security, and user authentication; and
5. gaining management's support for the project.

From this point on, we proceed to the particular issues of managing a CWIS: staffing, design, training, management, hardware, software, and maintenance. We hope that the reader also can generalize from these issues a set of principles that apply to any successful information management/automation project.

STAFF FOR THE CWIS

Generally, the CWIS manager is the person who organizes meetings, heads the planning task force, communicates with various offices, maintains the intellectual integrity of the system, and manages the data on the system. The CWIS system administrator is the person who manages the software and hardware that actually make the system run. In some organizations the CWIS manager will also be the CWIS system administrator. Given an exceptional person, this situation can be ideal in terms of control and personnel costs. Unfortunately, the talents required to perform these two jobs will rarely be found in a single individual. For most organizations, a partnership between the CWIS system administrator and the CWIS manager will be the most suitable arrangement. Again, a computer center system administrator and a librarian system manager can be an ideal combination.

If the task of providing and maintaining information is distributed to departments throughout the campus, then the manager and the system administrator can share in providing the necessary training in addition to monitoring the use of the service. In some larger organizations, additional IP trainers may be necessary and can be supervised by the CWIS manager. Having more than one person capable of providing training and monitoring the service allows for continuous management of the CWIS during vacations and illness.

The CWIS Project Manager

A CWIS is grown, not built. The key to a CWIS is information—information that is not static. If the service is not continuously enhanced, updated, and reviewed, it will cease to be of use to the campus. A CWIS is never done. In fact, the physical installation of the service is only a minor part of the overall project. The need for continuous information maintenance must be addressed at the beginning of the project. For some managers this continuous maintenance requirement can be new and potentially discomforting. The manager must be able to work with a broad range of IPs, keep them interested and trained, and ensure that the information being provided is of use to the campus. For some organizations this work can be a full-time job.

Often, establishing a CWIS is viewed as a computer project, and a computer specialist will be put in charge of seeing that the service is installed, tested, and documented. Unfortunately, this is only a fraction of what is required to make a CWIS work. The rest of the job involves coordinating IPs from many different departments, motivating them to continue to participate, and looking for new and interesting information that would be of use to the organization. If their experience has been limited to processing known information to answer specific, routine questions about matters like enrollment and student retention rates, computer specialists may be ill-suited for this part of the job. In fact, some will have no interest in performing these duties, and the service will suffer from their involvement. The CWIS manager should have experience with electronic information services, but does not need to be a programmer or systems administrator. The more important skills required are the ability to motivate a diverse group of people and the ability to coordinate a wide-ranging project that includes many types of information. The librarian, trained to be an information organizer, is the professional who can make the distribution system attractive to users by organizing it logically. So, he or she would be a natural choice as the CWIS manager.

Even the best manager needs sufficient time and resources to operate the service. If the CWIS is not seen as a living, growing thing, there may be an administrative tendency to place unrealistic completion dates on the activities of the people involved. The worst mistake a superior can make is to assign the manager additional projects just as the CWIS is installed and becomes available. It is at this point that the manager needs to be the most aggressive and spend the most time recruiting and training IPs from all across the campus. Additional assignments at this time limit the time the manager can spend keeping the service current and the IPs motivated. Information starts to become stale; IPs stop adding new information; users become dissatisfied with the service and management cannot figure out why. Managing a CWIS can be a full-time job for organizations with even a few hundred users—a fact that must be faced at the start of the project.

ESTABLISHING THE CWIS FOUNDATION

One of the most important aspects of starting a CWIS is establishing policies and procedures that will be acceptable to the campus community. One of the best ways to accomplish this campus-wide acceptance is to include a cross section of the campus in the planning process. The creation of a CWIS task force made up of people from various departments provides a means to bring together different viewpoints and knowledge of the information that can be made available. Just as administrative support for the CWIS is essential, reaching out into the organization for input and support is critical. Providing a way for departments to assist in the design and specification of the service gives them ownership of the project. These people become the frontline representatives of the service and can be used to stimulate interest throughout the rest of the organization. Without this type of support, the task facing the system manager will be monumental.

The Point of Entry

Key design decisions, such as the appearance of the point of entry to the service, should be worked out by the CWIS task force. CWIS experts agree that providing a stable point of entry for CWIS users is essential. Users can become disoriented when the point of entry changes, even if the changes are relatively minor and infrequent. In order to accomplish the necessary stability, a great deal of thought must be given to the design of the point of entry, the first screen. A task force with knowledge of the information to be made available and how this information will be used can design a point of entry that will remain useful for a long time.

One resource that must be included in the task force is librarians, people who are trained and practiced in organizing information in intuitive and meaningful ways. Their input will ensure that the structure of information will be useful to the campus community. At The University of Akron, the initial CWIS task force included five librarians: a combination of reference librarians, subject specialists, and public service managers. The task force may be established only to build the foundation of the CWIS and then dissolved, or it may be an ongoing group that reviews the service periodically and continues to provide input to the service manager.

Policies and Procedures

At The University of Akron, the CWIS policies and procedures were established by the CWIS task force. The task force wrote the first-level menu and decided that it must remain stable. The menu designs for the next level of menus were assigned to specific departments throughout campus. The task force also agreed on the need to maintain the currency of the data on the system. Feeling that it would be best to automate the process of maintaining data currency, the system administrator wrote a program that checks each file on the system for currency and warns the contributing IP by e-mail when the file is about to expire. The task force agreed to begin each file placed on the system with a header that specifies creation date, expiration date, contact person, and file title—all of which could be read by this currency-checker program. In this manner, data on the system is guaranteed to be current.

GETTING INFORMATION ON THE SERVICE

The job of providing and maintaining a large amount of information on a CWIS can be daunting. As we have said, for most organizations no single person is capable of doing this job. Distributing the responsibility for providing information is essential. The most efficient method of providing and maintaining this information is to allow the departments that ''own'' the information to be responsible. For example, in most organizations the purchasing department maintains the purchasing policies and procedures, and in turn can make these available on the CWIS. Changes to the policies or procedures can be updated as they are approved, making them available immediately. The purchasing department may eventually come to see the CWIS as the primary method of delivering information and promote its use throughout the organization. Distributing the responsibility for departmental information among the departments themselves is an effective and efficient means of getting a large amount of information on the service. This process also distributes the maintenance task. Departments that have a sense of ownership for their information will also be more comfortable with this arrangement. This practice, of course, means training and coordinating a large group of IPs.

Beginning Information Providers (IPs)

Training people to be IPs is a critical aspect of distributing the job of providing and maintaining information on the service—but it is not a simple matter. People chosen to be IPs for the departments can have widely varying capabilities and experience. Additionally, in many organizations, the hardware and software being used by various departments can be considerably different. Both of these aspects can complicate the job of training. One IP, for example, may transfer files across campus using the file transfer protocol (ftp) on the campus administrative network with one set of menus and commands, while another may use dial-in lines and a communication program. One may use a DOS machine, one a Macintosh, and another a Unix workstation. The manager must be able to train IPs in each of these environments.

Under such circumstances, individualized training may be the most effective way to prepare new IPs for the task. Individualized training can take place in the person's office, using familiar hardware and software. Practices and procedures learned this way will be more easily remembered. More time can be spent with people who have little computer experience, whereas more material can be covered with those that have more experience.

At The University of Akron, Gopher software was selected to run the CWIS. So, IPs are trained on how to produce and manipulate ASCII text files. Even though ASCII may not be the file format that they normally use, most learn readily to import and export ASCII text files to and from their word-processing software. They also must be trained how to write brief caption files that serve to build Gopher menus and how to transfer ASCII files across the campus network to the CWIS server, where the information ultimately resides.

IP Interaction

One way to keep IPs up-to-date and interested in the CWIS is to hold IP gatherings. These gatherings allow IPs to exchange experiences and discuss problems with others performing basically the same function; they can also be used as a forum for discussing policies and any compliance problems. Pertinent information—from that which indicates the number of user accesses to what information each IP has placed on the service—can be distributed. Possibly, awards for the most-accessed information can be made. These meetings should be more like pep rallies than lectures or evaluations.

Support for Advanced IPs

Most beginning training should concentrate on the basics of information formatting and information placement on the CWIS server. Some IPs will grow beyond these basics and desire more advanced access to the CWIS server. Some of the advanced capabilities IPs may wish to use include: the ability to link to other information available on the Internet, to build indexes of information for keyword searching, and to create interactive forms to collect information from users. Training must be available for these people to allow them to continue to develop their skills as IPs. Many IPs will need direct access to the CWIS server so that they may manipulate their information. Such training can be performed in a group, since the people receiving this type of training are already comfortable with the use of their own hardware and software.

The functions and features available on the CWIS server will evolve over time. As new functions and features become available, IPs will need to be trained on their use. Most system administrators will want to operate a separate test service in order to test new functions without affecting the production service. Advanced IPs should be given access to this test service to assist the administrator in determining which new functions and features are of value to the organization. Some features may be of use to even beginning IPs and should be incorporated into the training material they receive.

HARDWARE AND SOFTWARE

Most CWIS systems today are based on client-server architecture. This architecture provides high functionality by utilizing the capabilities of the desktop microcomputer systems that are pervasive today. In some cases, CWIS clients use multiuser, mainframe-type systems; however, these clients usually take advantage of only a portion of the capabilities of the microcomputer based clients.

The Gopher Selection

We chose the Gopher software developed at The University of Minnesota to run the CWIS for five reasons: (1) the client software is available for a wide range of computer systems, including IBM's VM/CMS operating system; (2) putting information on the Gopher server is comparatively simple for IPs with little computer experience; (3) there are thousands of Gopher servers worldwide from which our server could provide access to information outside our university; (4) both the client and server software are available at no cost to educational and nonprofit organizations; and (5) the Gopher software manages textual information, and because of infrastructure limitations, the CWIS had already been limited to textual information only.

The Client Side

CWIS users need access to a client system (workstation) equipped with the necessary application and network software. Systems with the necessary capabilities are available today for a few thousand dollars. A basic workstation consists of (1) a system unit with a microprocessor (Intel 486, Motorola 68040, or better), memory sized for the operating system and applications being used, hard disk, and a network interface (Ethernet, Token Ring, or LocalTalk de-pending on the network configuration); (2) a monitor, preferably color, sized for the needs of the user; (3) a keyboard and pointing device—mouse or trackball; (4) operating system software appropriate to the computer system being used; (5) network software appropriate to the network configuration; and (6) the CWIS client software. Simple VT-100 terminals can access a CWIS running Gopher software if they can reach a computer system like an IBM VM or a Digital Ultrix system that is running the appropriate Gopher client software.

The Server Side

A CWIS server system will also be necessary. Most CWIS server software operates with the Unix operating system. A wide variety of server systems that offer the Unix operating system are available at prices starting under $10,000. The University of Akron purchased a Digital DEC Alpha 3000/300LX with 32 megabytes of memory, built-in Ethernet adaptor, a 16-inch color monitor, 2 gigabytes of disk storage, a CD-ROM drive, and the OSF/1 operating system at an educational discount price of under $7,000.

Unix systems come with support for Transmission Control Protocol/Internet Protocol (TCP/IP) networking. Most CWIS systems utilize TCP/IP software. However, it may be necessary to enhance the organization's infrastructure to support TCP/IP. This enhancement could entail adding TCP/IP software to client workstations, LAN servers, or WAN routers. Network managers will need to learn to configure and maintain the TCP/IP software.

Infrastructure Concerns

There may also be a broad range of hardware capabilities across the organi-zation. A CWIS system that requires a great deal of resources, color graphics displays for example, may bypass users with older and less capable workstations. Other infrastructure considerations are also important. Users accessing the ser-vice remotely by telephone connections will have much slower transfer speeds, making services that transmit large amounts of information, like graphics, in-tolerably slow. Many campus networks may not be up to the task of providing this type of service. At The University of Akron, buildings are interconnected by a fiber-optic backbone. Telephone wiring is used to provide 10 megabits per second (Ethernet) connections to individual workstations within buildings. This infrastructure provides a campus network capable of delivering large amounts of information in reasonable lengths of time.

A Note About Users

Determining your users' skills and hardware capabilities is challenging and important. Consideration of the amount of training (and retraining) of users is essential. Most organizations will have users with a broad range of experience and capabilities. Some will have limited computer experience, or experience limited to different systems. Some will visit the CWIS infrequently, but they must be able to remember the necessary steps to access the service and navigate the information they find there. They may not be interested in investing a great deal of time to learn to use the service. These people must be able to access and use the service with a minimum of instruction or they will not use it. The service must be easy and consistent and provide hints and prompts to help the user along wherever possible. The Gopher software has a fairly effective built-in help system, although it may not be initially apparent to the user.

A basic design rule for menu-driven systems is to make every menu selection work as soon as it appears. Putting up menu selections for services that are not yet available can frustrate users. While building an empty framework for the CWIS menu structure may be a valuable paper exercise during the design stage, mounting that empty framework on the system can be disastrous. Once users see a system with lots of blank boxes indicating "nothing available," they will likely never return.

THE HARDWARE DENOMINATOR

We have mentioned the dangers of including data that requires the most sophisticated hardware. At the other extreme, allowing existing hardware capabilities to limit the type of information provided can serve to limit the system's growth and potential. There is a tendency to build services for the lowest common denominator. For many organizations, this denominator will be character terminals, or "dumb terminals." Indeed, at The University of Akron, the CWIS was limited to text-only information because of the broad installed base of text-only terminals. If the information actually needed by the organization requires greater capabilities, following this tendency to the lowest common denominator will be a mistake. An example would be not taking into account that a great many existing documents use multiple fonts and styles, have embedded graphics, and may even utilize color. The process of converting such information for the much simpler character terminal means losing all of the effort, and in some cases the actual content, that has been put into these documents.

It is clearly a difficult decision to chose a hardware and software environment for a CWIS that at once does not tie it to old technology, does not limit the service only to owners of high-end platforms, does not shut out important data formats, and does not require extensive training and overhead. We were faced with these conflicting issues—trying to accommodate the lowest common denominator while at the same time trying not to shut ourselves out of the future entirely. Our decision was to take a middle line in selecting the Gopher software. The Gopher system supports our broad installed base of VT100 and IBM 3270 terminals and does not limit the service to those with high-end workstations. It supports advanced capabilities, such as information linking, keyword indexing, and interactive forms. Although it does not provide graphics and multimedia, information on a Gopher server can be read with the more sophisticated World Wide Web browsers like Mosaic, which do run on high-end workstations. Additionally, the Gopher system requires a minimal amount of training to make IPs productive.

Evolving Toward the World Wide Web

Our campus is in the process of moving from terminals to desktop systems capable of graphics and multimedia. We have installed a World Wide Web server, which operates in parallel with our Gopher server. Many of the original CWIS task force members are learning to use Web browsers like Mosaic and Netscape. We see a natural evolution from terminal-based Gopher software, to Gopher clients that run on workstations, and on to Web browsers with advanced graphics and multimedia capabilities. This evolution will continue as more powerful CWIS systems become available and workstations become more capable.

Not providing workstations with adequate power for CWIS users can result in a shrunken user base. Some CWIS client software packages require substantial workstations in order to perform acceptably. For example, CWIS clients that support graphics, as do Mosaic and Netscape, require a much faster processor in the workstation as well as additional network bandwidth. When attempting to run such clients, workstations with limited capabilities will be unacceptably slow. If the workstations are not up to the task, users will be disappointed in the service and soon stop trying to use it. Once this happens, it will be difficult to regain these people as users, even when they have workstations capable of performing well.

Trying to run the service on an underpowered server can be another ingredient for failure. Just as important as having client workstations capable of doing the job, the server system must be able to perform with acceptable responsiveness. Today, server systems capable of servicing a large number of concurrent users are relatively inexpensive. Despite this fact, too often an existing system that does not have sufficient spare capacity to perform properly is pressed into providing the service. Slow response time will alienate users and result in the loss of users that will be hard to regain once the server system is upgraded. The small investment required for a first-rate server will yield a large return as the number of users and amount of information on the service both grow. Competition in the production of these types of systems is fierce, and many vendors are now producing systems with attractive price-performance ratios.

Existing Capabilities

Before estimating the cost of developing a CWIS, analyze the existing capabilities. If most potential CWIS users have access to systems that will allow the use of the selected CWIS software, the major cost of upgrading a large number of user systems can be avoided. If server hardware with sufficient power and storage is available for the selected CWIS software, the total cost will be that much smaller. The campus infrastructure, its data network, must be reviewed to ensure its capacity to handle the additional traffic created by a CWIS. This analysis should be performed after the analysis of the information to be provided, and after the initial selection (but before the purchase) of the appropriate CWIS software for the job. If the existing computing capabilities of the organization are allowed to drive all of the decisions as to information content on the CWIS, the long-term viability of the service may be jeopardized. The cost of enhancing systems and infrastructure may be worth the investment if the CWIS is to be of value to the entire organization.

CONTINUING COSTS

The largest continuing cost of the CWIS will be for staff if a full-time manager or administrator is needed. Hardware and software upgrades will be incremental and not substantial if the client and server systems have been chosen correctly; however, annual server hardware and software maintenance costs combined can total up to 24 percent of the purchase price.

CONCLUSION

A successful CWIS is carefully planned and managed. Hardware and software are chosen to fit the campus infrastructure and to handle the kinds of information that the CWIS must deliver. High-level administrative support encourages broad-based involvement in the design and maintenance of the service. The successful service is stable, current, easy to use, and available across the total variety of campus computing platforms. The service provides a natural opportunity for collaboration between the computer center and the library, and an opportunity for the library to extend its leadership role in the campus-wide delivery of information.

SELECTED BIBLIOGRAPHY

Boar, Bernard H. 1993. *The Art of Strategic Planning for Information Technology: Crafting Strategy for the 90s.* New York: John Wiley & Sons.

Kochner, Jonathan, and NorthWestNet. 1993. ''Campus Wide Information Systems (CWIS).'' In *Internet Passport: NorthWestNet's Guide to Our World Online.* Bellevue, Wash.: NorthWestNet and Northwest Academic Computing Consortium, Inc., pp. 295–306.

Liu, Cricket et al. 1994. *Managing Internet Information Services.* Sebastopol, Calif.: O'Reilly & Associates, Inc.

Lloyd, Les, ed. 1992. *Campus-Wide Information Systems and Networks: Case Studies in Design and Implementation.* Westport, Conn.: Meckler.

Regan, Elizabeth A., and Bridget N. O'Connor. 1994. *End-User Information Systems: Perspectives for Managers and Information Systems Professionals.* New York: Macmillan.

Robson, Wendy. 1994. *Strategic Management and Information Systems: An Integrated Approach.* London: Pitman.

Wiggins, Richard W. 1994. "Building a Campus-Wide Information System." *Campus-Wide Information Systems (CWIS)* 11(1–2): 57–66.

5

Too Many Concerns? Paper or Online, Local or Remote, Full Text or Index

Margaret Sylvia

The proliferation of new electronic databases and search engines is delivering a host of new choices for librarians and system administrators. The problems presented by these choices are particularly difficult ones for small- and medium-sized academic libraries. Previously, one only had to decide what paper indexes to purchase and then whether the indexes were affordable. Now many indexes are available in a wide variety of formats so that the choices to be made have become much more complex. In addition, much more than single indexing has become available. Full-text online, on CD-ROM, or by document delivery is now an option to be considered as well. How can a useful decision be made among all the options now available? Librarians must consider the needs of the users as well as the options and budget available.

BUDGETING FOR RESOURCES: PAPER OR ELECTRONIC

A balance must be struck between the money that will be spent for online sources and that which will go to traditional paper sources. More and more libraries are canceling paper indexes in order to subscribe to an electronic version. When an index is made available in electronic version, the print version gets very little use as a rule. Cancellation of paper indexes was almost unheard of in libraries even a few years ago for a number of reasons. Academic librarians were suitably nervous about accreditation for various programs where subscriptions to certain indexes were required. Today, when students and faculty are given appropriate access to the electronic version, paper indexes are not required for accreditation by most accrediting bodies. One small academic library in the San Antonio area made a dramatic change in its collection by dropping many journal and index subscriptions and allocating the money to a full-text CD-ROM system. This system is very popular with the students, but it is a single-user workstation and would not be a workable solution for a larger library, unless the dozens of CD-ROMs containing the full-text journal images were networked.

When extra funds are difficult to come by, as they are in most small libraries, current budgets must be reallocated in order to fund different materials. One way to consider allocating the budget is to institute electronic indexes on a trial basis and then study the use made of the electronic index and the paper index by the students. If twice as much use is made of electronic indexes as paper ones, the funds might be allocated such that twice as much of the index budget goes to electronic indexes as to paper indexes. A similar argument might be made for budgeting of full-text materials in online and in paper format.

Until recently, small college librarians were also wary of the inherent unreliability of computers and computer networks. Card catalogs and paper indexes never ''go down'' and so were much more trustworthy than computer-based resources. When electronic access is unavailable for long periods and at unpredictable times, good reference service requires a backup. This predicament kept many libraries subscribing to paper indexes along with the electronic counterparts. There is no substitute for reliability and if downtime is excessive and unplanned, the computer system needs closer examination. Appropriate downtime for maintenance and upgrades can be anticipated as part of normal operations, and the library should plan to be closed for major upgrades. In some cases, nights and weekends may be the time of choice for shutdowns on the grounds that fewer users will be adversely affected. Proper maintenance is most helpful in ensuring reliability, and upgrades are a necessary part of computer maintenance. When these caveats are followed, the improved reliability of current computer technology makes uncontrolled downtime less of a risk.

Most electronic databases are not available for purchase as paper indexes are; they can only be leased. Access to them is totally available or totally unavailable unlike paper indexes, which, once purchased, are owned by the library and are not returned if the subscription is canceled. Some librarians want to have physical materials to show for their expenditures, and these services provide nothing that can be retained. In most cases, nothing is left to store if a cancellation is made. However, CD-ROMs offer much better searching and take up very little space. They can, however, only be searched by one person at a time while multivolume paper indexes can be shared by several patrons. This limitation of CD-ROMs can be corrected, at a cost, by multiple subscriptions or by computer network access.

It is time to make intelligent collection development choices and select appropriate formats rather than simply duplicate resources. It has been our experience that if the network is unavailable, people do not use the paper indexes. They ask when the network will be in service and return to do their research then. We also find that people prefer to use an electronic index even if it is not appropriate to their needs, rather than a paper index that is appropriate. For example, many of our users, in researching topics for religious studies, will use the computerized *Humanities Index* on our network instead of choosing the paper *Catholic Periodical Index* or *Religion Index*. *Humanities Index* is an excellent resource, but the other titles clearly give better subject coverage. We need to compensate for these poor choices in our bibliographic instruction program by demonstrating how an online index, while easier to use, is not always the best choice for the user.

In order to take advantage of electronic resources, the library must have in place a reliable method of doing so and a budgetary plan for purchasing the electronic resources as well as the hardware needed. Many of the indexes used in libraries have become widely available in many different formats, so a library that makes them available electronically must consider dropping the paper subscription when enough computer access is available. Often, however, the cancellation of print indexes will not cover the price of a substitute computer index, so other funds must be made available. Many libraries have simply reassigned funds from existing book and journal budgets, while others have attempted to increase their budgets using the need for electronic resources as justification. Again, usage is the key and collecting usage statistics is very important for justifying budget requests. When an index strongly supports one or more disciplines that are important at a college, and it is used heavily by students, it should be purchased. Online or CD-ROM indexes save time and can produce better results; librarians must make decisions about funding based on concrete evidence of needs and usage. Keeping usage statistics online and sampling the use of paper indexes will provide the necessary information to help make decisions and justify budget requests.

Many academic administrators assume that money can be saved by accessing electronic resources, rather than by purchasing printed materials. This is usually a false assumption. First, equivalent electronic resources are generally far more expensive than their print counterparts. Second, the vast majority of recorded information is not yet available electronically. This is true for full-text book and journal resources, although computerized access to full-text materials is increasing rapidly. Traditional paper publishing is not withering away; on the contrary, it seems to flourish. Further, due to the fear by publishers of copyright infringement as well as other problems, much of this newly published material will not be available in electronic format in the near future. Several hundred years of published materials are also unavailable in electronic format. Electronic publishing is not going to eliminate the need for printed textual material, although it will reduce the need for searching through individual volumes of paper indexes.

REMOTE OR LOCAL ACCESS

Once the decision is made to purchase a particular resource in electronic format, consideration turns to the variety of formats available. For some databases, there is only one choice, but this is becoming the exception rather than the rule: should the database be locally mounted or made available by searching a remote site? Locally mounted databases require more local expertise as well as more local resources, such as hard disk space and processor power. Alternatively, remote resources are subject to high connect charges and sometimes to connection problems. These problems are exacerbated when indexes are accessed over the Internet. The best resources may become very difficult to access and use when Internet traffic is heavy. One would never wish to depend solely on Internet access for a heavily used resource. Library management may need to consider using a local area network and having a predictably heavily used index (i.e., ERIC) mounted on its own system.

Any sort of remote access should be verified for costs, reliability, and accessibility over a period of time. Remote access is probably most useful for lesser-used indexes though it may also be the best answer for all electronic access in small libraries without the expertise or money to build and maintain a large in-house computer system for local database access. There are a variety of remote database options available at the present time, including UnCover from CARL for journal indexing and the FirstSearch database service from OCLC. Telnet access on the Internet is currently free to UnCover, and the number and variety of periodicals covered is very large, though the searching capabilities are somewhat limited. There is also no actual indexing done on this database since it uses only the article title, author, journal title, and abstract terms as access points. Custom gateways are available for a fee. Ebsco offers a competing online product, Casius, which presents much the same information as UnCover, i.e., keyword searching of journal tables of contents. It is more expensive but offers better searching capabilities.

Access to FirstSearch is available either by purchasing blocks of a specified number of searches or through individual passwords that allow unlimited searching for a year. FirstSearch allows access to a collection of databases, which are generally well indexed as opposed to only allowing keyword searching of journals' tables of contents. A distinct advantage of FirstSearch over other collections of individual databases is the common search interface, which is fairly user-friendly. However, it can be much more expensive than the other alternatives. Dialog is an important source of online databases with a common search interface; however, the pricing structure of this service places it out of reach of most libraries for end-user searching. Usually, this service has been reserved for library-mediated searching, often with part or all the charges being borne by the individual user. Library service plans should include a standard for when mediated searching is preferred and when end-user searching is preferred. Mediated searching is usually used for expensive search services. Flat fees for unlimited searching of databases are more easily budgeted for by libraries than for end-user searching.

LOCAL ELECTRONIC ACCESS: CD-ROM OR TAPE-LOAD

For most libraries, the best option for heavily used databases is local access, assuming the library and its parent institute are able and willing to invest the money necessary to build and maintain the supporting infrastructure. In this case, the choice of databases can be made in the library and by using traditional collection development guidelines: which users does the library support and what are their needs? In colleges, both circulation and use of current indexes are usually good guidelines. However, evaluate current use with caution since some indexes are difficult to use in paper format and thus are used less; they may be much easier to use in electronic format. There are also databases available that have no paper counterpart; they exist only in electronic form.

Local access to databases can be divided into access via tape-load or CD-ROM. Tape-loads of data on the disk drives of local public access catalogs have the advantage of giving a common interface for all databases, which is a considerable blessing. End-user training time is vastly simplified, reducing the workload for librarians. Tape-loads also have the advantage of being searchable in one pass; CD-ROM databases are often split into more than one disk and, in many cases, multiple disks cannot be searched at the same time. The online catalog computer must have vastly increased disk space to hold multiple tape-loaded databases as well as increased power to process complex searches and return the answer in a reasonable time. As a rule, CD-ROM access time is slower than that for accessing data stored on a hard disk—although the time spent on either search will vary depending on the processing power of the computer, the complexity of the search, the size of the database, and other variables.

The blessing of the common search interface of the public catalog can be a limitation. Often the CD-ROM search software is carefully matched to the database, thus providing powerful search capabilities. Many online public catalogs, however, offer only author, title, subject, and keyword access, plus the boolean operators "and," "or," and perhaps "not." The specialized search software of CD-ROMs often allows much more intricate search capability. For instance, one may wish to limit the search by year of publication, and then search material only in particular journal titles, or search only thesaurus terms. CD-ROM search software is generally well suited to the database it is paired with. Often, OPAC search software leaves much to be desired when it is used for searching journal indexes, because of its more limited searching options.

If a decision is made to purchase CD-ROM databases, a variety of choices must be faced. For example, will the CD-ROMs be placed on stand-alone work stations or will they be networked? Here the trade-offs are cost and access. Networks are more costly, but they allow several patrons to search at once.

While the trend in the industry seems to be toward unlimited access for networked databases, there are some publishers who base charges on the number of simultaneous users on a network, the number of workstations attached, or the total number of possible users of the database. Such restrictions can place a severe burden on the network administrator who must remain within the contract requirements and within the budget available.

It is preferable to decide which indexes will be most needed in the library, and then consider purchasing the CD-ROM product that is common to most of them. This will mean a single, main computer interface and will reduce end-user training time and librarians' training workload. Many indexes are now being introduced that have no paper equivalent; so if the library is considering replacing a particular paper index, close equivalents should be considered. Typical near equivalents often contain much more information than the printed index. When purchasing indexes of any type, librarians must consider their library's journal holdings and the holdings of nearby libraries, if users are able to access them. Even with high-speed fax machines and overnight document delivery, local holdings are still most convenient for users.

Other factors to consider in choosing a CD-ROM search product include ease of use for end users, memory requirements at the workstation, network installation and security requirements, the possibility of adding local holdings statements to the data, and the stability of the software. Search interfaces that are difficult for end users to grasp make a heavy workload for librarians. Software installation requirements can be a big problem, particularly for CD-ROM networking. Many CD-ROM systems allow users to exit to DOS, which can create a problem in networks. Others may require the capability to write temporary files to a particular network directory; some must be installed in the root directory; some require that particular software be installed on the workstation, such as a DOS "share" program or DOS extensions. Some are unstable in a network environment and "freeze up" periodically for no apparent reason. One of the biggest problems for CD-ROM networking is having enough available memory in each workstation to run the search engine. Some interfaces require only a minimal amount of conventional memory, while others require large amounts. Though workstations may have several megabytes of expanded and/or extended memory, DOS programs are still restricted by the first 640K of memory. Even with appropriate memory management, this can be a problem when the operating system and all the network drivers are loaded. Slow access time for CD-ROMs can sometimes be remedied by copying the database to a hard disk on the network server, if the producer allows this and if there is a large enough disk drive available. Copying the database consumes time and processor resources while it is being accomplished, but it provides some of the advantages of a tape-load onto an OPAC, and typically at lower costs.

FULL TEXT AND DOCUMENT DELIVERY

Getting the full text of a journal article, as opposed to simply the indexing and bibliographic information, is usually the goal of the researcher. When the library makes good indexing available in electronic format, it is much easier for the researcher to collect a large bibliography of useful citations. This increases the use of and requests for full-text materials. There are a number of ways to satisfy these needs in addition to the traditional methods of journal subscriptions in paper, microfilm or microfiche, or interlibrary loan. Some vendors such as University Microfilms International (UMI), Ebsco, and Infotrac are introducing ASCII full-text searchable journal and newspaper articles. Again, the library will often have a choice of whether to use remote, tape-load, or CD-ROM access for this. Most of the same considerations apply to this as to the decision on purchasing indexes in the three formats.

One drawback to these full-text databases is that most graphics, such as charts, graphs, and pictures are often absent. Searching a full-text database requires end-user training so users do not waste time and become frustrated browsing through hundreds of items that are only peripherally related to their searches. Full-text journal article access is also available in another slightly different format on CD-ROM from at least one vendor, UMI, through its ProQuest product. This access includes a traditional index to the articles on CD-ROM with links to "photos" or graphic images of the full text on another set of CD-ROMs. In this case, the full text is not searchable since it is present only in graphic format; however, all graphics are included in the product. Full-text access, however, tends to be fairly expensive regardless of format or vendor. The price for over-night document delivery during a test run of CARL and FirstSearch averaged $10–$12 per article.

Document-delivery services are an expensive option for fast delivery of full-text material. The table-of-contents services mentioned above, including those from FirstSearch, Ebsco, and CARL, all promise quick delivery of full-text journal articles. Sometimes these can be delivered within an hour by fax, while most promise same day or overnight delivery. All copyright fees are paid by the vendor and are included in the charge to the buyer of the service.

If remote access to databases by end users is seen as a separate step from document delivery, the ease of end-user searching, speed of access, and avail-ability of appropriate journals in the database could be evaluated most strongly, with delivery capabilities as a secondary consideration. If document delivery is a primary process following end-user searching on locally held databases, then cost, reliability, and speed of delivery should be considered more strongly as factors in the decision-making process of choosing a document-delivery vendor.

MANAGEMENT DECISIONS

There are many factors that must be developed in the library plan for service and must be considered when final decisions are made regarding the purchase of indexes as well as full-text materials in various formats. The first five factors listed below are specific to choosing indexes, however, and the remainder apply to both indexes and full-text materials.

Collection Development Considerations
    Number of titles indexed
    Number of years covered
    Library holdings of titles indexed
    Indexing coverage (full or selective)
    Indexing quality
    Library holdings of other local libraries
    Curriculum subjects focus (research/writing or lab/classroom)
    Number of undergraduate students in the subject area
    Number of graduate students in the subject area
    Number of faculty doing research in the subject area
    Number of research-intensive assignments in the subject area

User Needs
    Scholarly research or casual use
    Ease of use
    Speed of access
    Availability to concurrent users
    Training needs of users
    Anticipated level of use (heavy or light)
    Anticipated level of downtime or unavailability

Cost Considerations
    Training needs of librarians
    Hardware needs
    Space needs
    Personnel needs (reference assistance, system maintenance, system administration, and so on)
    Supply needs (shelving, filing, paper, ink or toner, and so on)
    Cost to the library
    Cost to the user
    Security requirements

There is no one correct answer to the problems of database and document access for every library and every user. Each library must be evaluated according to the goals it sets for itself and the needs of its users. The factors discussed above should be considered for each database, balanced against the advantages and disadvantages in different types of access. Each access decision that is made has repercussions on every other decision. It is necessary for librarians and system administrators to evaluate current access decisions against those made previously, in terms of new choices that may make a different mix of products a superior solution.

FUTURE VISIONS

When planning for future access, consider the direction your library is taking, the needs of your users, the options available, and the budget. Should you spend more on document delivery and less on journal subscriptions? Should you be receiving your full-text journal subscriptions on paper, microfilm, microfiche, or CD-ROM, or via online from a remote database? What choices will be available next year that may change everything? While planning for the future in a rapidly changing environment might seem almost impossible, it is still very important. You should develop vision of the direction your library will take and continue to develop that vision.

REFERENCES

Cibarrelli, Pamela, Elliot H. Gertel, and Mona Kratzert. 1993. "Choosing Among the Options for Patron Access Databases: Print, Online, CD-ROM, or Locally Mounted." *Reference Librarian* 39: 85–97.

Piety, John. 1992. "The Anatomy of a Decision: Tape vs. CD-ROM—Which Product and Why?" *Online* 16 (September): 62–65.

Richman, Barry. 1993. "Online or Ondisc? When to Choose CD-ROM for your Database." *CD-ROM Professional* 6 (March): 53–54.

Sylvia, Margaret, and Marcella Lesher. 1994. "Making Hard Choices: Cancelling Print Indexes." *Online* 18(1): 59–65.

PART II

Technical Services in Academic Libraries

The six chapters in Part II of our book deal with automation in technical services. A major theme is the bibliographic database. Changing from cards to computers has been neither simple nor cheap and many mistakes have been made along the way (in Chapter 11, Cassandra Brush covers some of those old mistakes and why we made them). One of our favorite clichés in libraries is: "Yes, building an electronic database is very expensive but it's a long-term investment in our future and that justifies the costs." We are learning, however, that maintenance costs can make that investment even more expensive. Catalog databases deteriorate with age. As cataloging rules, rule interpretations, classification codes, subject headings, and Machine Readable Cataloging formats evolve, old records become obsolete. We'd like them to be fully modern, something we often neglected in card and book catalogs.

The core problem here is one we have always had to deal with in library automation. Library staff might have to work with a card catalog containing records prepared over a 50-year span. Often staff and public cope with this reasonably well. This success happened because all kinds of informal but workable judgments. We haven't taught library computers to be very good at informal judgments or coping with the kind of variations and inconsistencies we used to tolerate in card catalogs. Librarians can use all the help available in maintaining bibliographic databases while containing costs.

In Chapter 6, Stephen P. Foster and Maryhelen Jones bring together two topics not usually associated, technical services and off-campus programs. Typically, reader services bears the responsibility for supporting off-campus students and faculty. Clearly, that shouldn't be the case. Central Michigan University established an off-campus unit in its library in 1976. As this chapter explains, that unit has worked to provide innovative services to off-campus programs for nearly two decades with technical services in an important role. Establishing a special unit and budgeting resources has allowed technical services to provide special services to off-campus programs.

Susan E. Ketcham examines the choices for locating MARC formatted records from alternate resources in Chapter 7. Her chapter is partially based on a survey of more than one hundred libraries. Many mid-sized and larger libraries have relied heavily on the major bibliographic utilities, but there are other choices; Ms. Ketcham describes them and the trade-offs involved in using them.

In Chapter 8, Christine E. Thompson first reviews sources for bibliographic records: the bibliographic utilities, CD-ROM databases, and disks or tapes supplied by jobbers. She next discusses costs, cost calculation methods, and cost containment. She also discusses changes in workflow and quality control methods that can be varied to maintain acceptable quality within tolerable budgets. Finally, she looks at staffing and staff development.

Elaine Sanchez provides a detailed account in Chapter 9 of managing the change to a first automated system and of retaining the knowledge from that experience, which will assist the later transition from a first system to a second and a second to a third. Her university, Southwest Texas State University (STSU), began preparation for their first automation system in 1987. Detailed planning and a project management structure allowed STSU to make a relatively smooth transition, including database conversion.

Maintaining a high-quality database while controlling costs is the central theme of Chapter 10 by Myrtle Joseph and Nancy C. Fricke. Some of the options discussed are: re-engineering workflow, the trade-off between spending on staff and on technology, "outsourcing," reducing bibliographic utility costs, and original cataloging, among others. Their chapter is a veritable catalog of options.

Cassandra Brush, in Chapter 11, discusses database integrity. An important part of her chapter is the story of how many catalogers in the early days of the Online Computer Library Center played all kinds of clever tricks with the system. Some of these tricks saved time and money, but left many errors on the library's archival tape; errors, however, that didn't show on the printed cards that were produced. These errors, Ms. Brush warns us, can reappear as very unpleasant surprises when a library loads the archival tapes on an automation system. Her chapter tells us what to watch for and how to avoid similar problems reoccurring.

6

Managing Technical Services Support for Off-Campus Library Programs

Stephen P. Foster and Maryhelen Jones

INTRODUCTION

Information technology is making a far-reaching, revolutionary impact on higher education. Vice President Al Gore has drawn public attention to the Internet—the Information Superhighway, as it has popularly come to be known—and speculation about its social and political significance is appearing in such varied publications as *The New Republic* and *The National Review*. In a recent *Chronicle of Higher Education* interview, Douglas Van Houwelin, Vice-Provost for Information Technology at the University of Michigan, states the implications clearly and emphatically: "Universities are about sharing knowledge and information, and what we're seeing now [with personal computing and networking] is about the same thing. The convergence here is going to be something we can't imagine" (Jacobson 1994: A26). The impact of information technology on libraries and library services is likewise difficult to imagine, a fact that makes planning and decision making particularly challenging for managers and administrators.

One does, however, feel confident in predicting a period of rapid expansion for "distance education" (distance education allows education to take place at remote sites by using such technologies as television and telecommunications) and the library services needed to support it. Modern telecommunicating technology has diluted the concentration of just about everything, including political and economic power, and it also tends to bring about the decentralization of organizations (Huber 1994: 50). Large, centralized, hierarchical educational bureaucracies will be rendered less necessary as information becomes even more portable and transferrable. The Open University in the United Kingdom, with more than 200,000 students and with liaisons to similar institutions in Finland, Portugal, and Greece, may help to give a glimpse of the international future of distance education. More students will be taking courses and completing degree programs without ever stepping onto a traditional campus or sitting in a conventional college classroom or lecture hall. Competition in distance education is intense and will become even more so as technological developments open new possibilities. The traditional university or college library must provide the essential support for the traditional campus educational mission, and so the development of off-campus educational programs and the teaching of off-campus courses requires well-planned library support (McCabe 1986: 172–189).

It is reasonable to conclude then that just as colleges and universities will be dramatically altered by emerging information technology with its vast potential for sharing information and knowledge, so also will libraries and library services. Demand for services will escalate as technological innovations create new possibilities and raise service expectations. Thoughtful, informed planning and careful decision making are key managerial elements that will enable libraries to strengthen the educational institutions they support as they undergo these extraordinary transformations.

So much of the difficult-to-imagine change ahead of us is technology-driven. All institutions, but particularly educational institutions, will define themselves in large part through the creativity of their use of technical resources. Information technology, however, is costly, complex, and constantly changing. Without solid, cost-effective technical services support, a library's public service programs will suffer. Therefore, the decision-making and planning processes that determine the application of information technology to technical services operations in support of off-campus library programs are of critical importance both in terms of cost and of service. ("Technical services," for the purposes of this chapter, refers to acquisitions, cataloging, authority-control work, and automated-systems operations.)

From a managerial-service perspective, technical services support for a library's public service programs is a critical question with major programmatic implications. This is certainly the case with off-campus library programs. The success of any library program rests heavily on the judicious determination of what configurations of technical services support make cost-efficient use of moderately scarce institutional resources. A library prospers in so far as it can deliver high-quality services. And, the capacity to deliver these services comes from a complex infrastructure of automation. While each off-campus library program is unique and has its own institutional framework and culture within which to operate, it is nevertheless valuable to examine managerial decision-making and planning factors that pertain to general technical services issues. Also, while the focus of this chapter is on off-campus library programs, the analysis and observations have a broader and more general application.

The Central Michigan University Off-Campus Library Services program functions in this chapter as a model with which to analyze issues and make observations that are relevant to successful managerial decision making and planning for technical services. Central Michigan University's OCLS program is among the oldest, continuously running programs of its kind in the United States, originating in 1976. OCLS is an academic support service for The College of Extended Learning, Extended Degree Programs. About 90 percent of the 12,000 annual course enrollments are at the graduate level. The program is staffed by seven professional librarians plus seven support members and student assistants. Library services include document delivery, reference assistance, bibliographic instruction, mediated computerized database searching, guided end-user searching, and the creation of course-related instructional materials (bibliographies, research guides, and so on).

This chapter considers three general areas of administrative or managerial concern that relate to technical services support for off-campus library programs. All three concerns are tied up with important, interlinked issues of cost and service. The delivery of innovative off-campus library services, relying heavily as it does on computing and telecommunications technology, is directly related to the quality of the supporting technical services operations. Technical services operations are costly in terms both of personnel and equipment. The first area of concern deals with the acquisition and cataloging of off-campus library materials. The second discusses technical support issues related to the provision of electronic, online services. The third deals with the automation infrastructure for document delivery.

Maintenance Issues

Because almost all library services are highly automation-dependent, most cost and service decisions involve important and complex automation-application issues. Some general considerations, however, should be kept in mind when planning automation purchases. First is the hardware and software maintenance factor. In addition to the initial cost-outlay for new computer and telecommunications systems, there is the ongoing maintenance cost, usually estimated to run around 15 percent of the initial purchase price. In long-range budget planning, it is important to remember that simply accounting for the purchase of automation itself is not enough: the ongoing cost of maintenance must be factored in. Maintenance, though, is often a negotiable cost. Such strategies as waving maintenance charges for a period of time or locking in a maximum percentage increase are a couple of commonly negotiated possibilities. Library administrators must educate funding officers on the complexities and slipperiness of maintenance issues. It is also important to remember that the incremental upgrading of hardware and software will drive up maintenance costs. The purchase of additional disk drives, for example, or upgrading a processor will add to ongoing maintenance fees.

Obsolescence Factor

Maintenance costs are part of another consideration—the obsolescence factor. Rapid developments in computer technology and the intensely competitive automation market virtually assure that hardware and software life is shortened by vendors limiting or withdrawing support when new models or versions are introduced. Current hardware and software adequacy and effectiveness should be evaluated frequently (annually if possible). Memory, software, and peripheral upgrades as well as system replacements should be a part of the budget.

Personnel

Personnel is another critical, undeniable important factor. The current trend in computing and data communications of distributed processing means that managers will be faced with the challenge of supplying increasingly sophisticated systems administration and support. Highly trained technical personnel are expensive to compensate, and frequently difficult to find, recruit, and retain. Increasingly sophisticated systems also mean that the demand for staff training will rise and remain omnipresent. Software upgrades frequently change functionality, which in turn creates the need for additional training. Training costs will rise either in the form of permanent staff as trainers or in the form of contracted trainers.

These considerations, of course, have major funding and budget implications, and it is particularly important not to lose sight of them. An institution's senior leadership likes to hear about the wonderful things that the new, expensive automation will do (along with the impressive price tags come high expectations); but, the issues of training, personnel, maintenance, rapid obsolescence, and amortization are less popular discussion topics. Yet all of these are vitally important aspects of planning for technical services.

ACQUISITIONS-CATALOGING SUPPORT FOR OFF-CAMPUS SERVICES

The timely acquisition of library materials as well as their efficient and accurate cataloging are operations critical to the success of any library, traditional or off-campus. Decision making and planning efforts in this area must consider the level of support available from the host or supporting institution, the feasibility and desirability of maintaining separate collections, and the possible advantages that might come from "outsourcing" the technical services functions of acquisitions and cataloging.

Integrated In-House Technical Support

For an off-campus library program that is attached to a long-established, well-supported parent or host institution with trained technical services personnel, operations such as cataloging and acquisitions can be integrated into the routine operation of the main library. With equipment and trained staff in place, the addition of off-campus materials to the main library's workflow is seamless—adding little additional expense compared with the cost of setting up and maintaining a separate dedicated operation. Integrated online library systems have the capacity to create and support separate holdings locations with relative ease; therefore, materials can easily be processed for placement and maintenance in a separate collection with a separate circulation system.

The OCLS program at Central Michigan University uses the integrated model of acquisitions-cataloging support described above. The ordering, processing, and cataloging of library materials is performed as an integrated part of the technical services operations by the technical services staff of the Central Michigan University Libraries. OCLS has a separate acquisitions budget for monographs and serials, and separate fund codes for establishing audit trails; however, the ordering, processing, cataloging, and authority-control work for its purchased materials is part of the general technical services process. This enables the program to realize the cost benefits from volume-discount buying and to take advantage of the efficiencies of a relatively large technical services staff and library automation infrastructure. The materials purchased by OCLS are also integrated into the main library collection with no OCLS purchase attribution. Thus collection integration results in a two-way level of support: OCLS-selected materials enrich the main library's collection, while the entire main library collection becomes available to the off-campus student and faculty member while away from the campus.

Out-of-House Technical Support

A practical workable alternative to the integrated model in acquisitions and cataloging (above) is "outsourcing." Outsourcing is the contracting of traditionally in-house technical services functions such as acquisitions, cataloging, and authority control to commercial vendors. The invention of MARC (Machine Readable Cataloguing) approximately 25 years ago, along with remarkable innovations in telecommunications and computing, resulted in an enormously beneficial standardization of bibliographic information formats. These developments have made bibliographic information into a highly manipulable, interchangeable, and portable commodity. This "new product" has spawned a plethora of commercialized vending services that provide the technical services operations of acquisitions, cataloging, and authority control. These now aggressively compete with the traditional in-house technical services departments. Competition is increasing, and it is reasonable to expect that prices will go down. Here we see a rather remarkable example of the decentralizing impact of information technology. Outsourcing, in some cases, provides cost-efficient alternatives to traditional in-house technical services operations. The Online Computer Library Center (OCLC) in Dublin, Ohio, is one vendor that offers cataloging and technical processing services.

The decision to outsource is a complicated one with many complex cost factors to consider. Acquisitions and cataloging functions are labor-intensive, high-cost, high-overhead operations. First and foremost is the consideration of the level and adequacy of the current acquisitions and cataloging support. Central Michigan University's extended degree programs (EDP) concentrate on offering administrative, health care, and education courses. These areas of study are technology-driven. Adequate library support involves the rapid purchase and processing of relevant monographs, serials, and other materials. Timeliness of data and research is extremely important. Students and the faculty who teach them require library materials and information resources that are current, up-to-date, and readily available. Also many off-campus courses, as well as traditional campus courses, are short, lasting only three to six weeks. Taking classes in a compressed format makes efficient, rapid turnaround in cataloging and acquisitions even more imperative from an end user's perspective. There is simply no time for expensive, much-needed materials to sit, unavailable, on processing or cataloging backlog shelves, or for orders to wend their way slowly through a clogged acquisitions queue. Off-campus students (many of whom are working adults) who cannot get what they need will find other supply sources—the most dramatic being educational programs at other institutions.

Considerations

It is important then for off-campus library program managers to look carefully at the turnaround time for materials and to monitor closely satisfaction levels of library patrons with services, particularly with respect to timeliness. Cataloging and acquisitions time studies are one way to assess the effectiveness of technical services support in terms of decreasing the turnaround time in making newly acquired resources available.

The consideration of outsourcing makes sense if: in-house support is wavering or inadequate; budgetary pressures are reducing technical services staffing and support; or the library materials require specialized or customized cataloging or processing. Responses to requests for information (RFIs) and requests for proposals (RFPs) will provide some basis for cost comparisons and for assurance of quality control. Vendors will offer specific turnaround times for delivery of cataloged material. Limited or selective outsourcing may also be a cost-effective option. Selective outsourcing might be advantageous when the materials purchased are of such a nature that in-house staff lacks expertise to perform the appropriate tasks. For example, materials in esoteric languages or in specialized formats, such as computer files or audiovisual tapes might fall into this category.

With the relentless digitalization of all kinds of information, electronic formats for information are exploding. Electronic serials and hypertext documents will present a new set of bibliographic challenges. Nevertheless, bibliographical and authority control will be extremely important operations for providing systematic access to the new electronic formats. With the enormous proliferation of information resources, maintaining bibliographic control becomes a vital function in making the new information technology a boon rather than a bane. How this is to be done and by whom are not easy questions to answer. It is safe to say that acquisitions, cataloging, and bibliographic control will be transformed in the next few years.

ONLINE INFORMATION SERVICES

Creative methods of providing online access to information is a paramount feature of planning and decision making for library managers and administrators. "Access versus ownership" is an important catchphrase that captures what is turning out to be a profound normative shift for the institutional role of libraries. In effect, technological changes force the questions: What should libraries be? What kinds of services should they offer? How should these services be evaluated and reevaluated? How are these services to be financed? How can personnel most effectively and efficiently provide these services? The future capacity of even the largest research institutions to fund traditional library acquisitions programs has dramatically diminished and will continue to do so. The rapid proliferation of all sorts of intellectual material, their spiraling costs, and the cost limitations of storage are the major reasons why the wealthiest libraries will not be able to own even a substantial percentage of the material needed and demanded by their patrons. Also, materials or documents in paper, microfiche, or any other nondigitized format are not as portable as those in digitized form—and portability is becoming an increasingly important feature of information. The digitalization of information radically transforms the whole question of ownership of library documents and materials. "Libraries," as one recent article puts it, "have been forced to move from owning materials to accessing materials on a 'just in time' basis" (Goodyear and Dodd 1994: 253). Drawn from the business world's interest in the cost efficiency of inventory supply maintenance, that short phrase reflects both the economic and technological shifts with regard to funding models for libraries as well as pointing to shifting roles and expectations.

The "versus" in the phrase stresses the fact that this is a library management *decision* issue. The dichotomy suggests how critical managerial planning is: Do library managers put their relatively scarce dollars into collections or into information-access technology? Or do they establish a rationale and percentage of dollars for assessing both categories?

The dichotomy perhaps is overworked—collections are not going to disappear completely. But the rapid development of information technology and the obsolescence factor make the planning process a classical case of decision making in the face of uncertainty. The level of uncertainty, to be sure, is high and often stressful.

Challenges and Opportunities of Off-Campus Programs

Because off-campus library programs are so much involved with supporting students over long distances, they present special challenges and unique opportunities for exploring innovative approaches to the delivering of information-access services. The rapid development of the Internet, with its vast information resources, now makes the *location* of the student an irrelevant factor; this is a quite revolutionary change when you stop to think of it. Such a change may make the notion of an educational institution as a place where a student *goes* obsolete (Perelman 1992: 51–65). The value of the Internet with its worldwide connections to information resources to off-campus library programs is quickly becoming obvious. Over the next few years its impact on library services will be enormous.

Central Michigan University's OCLS program is supported by an infrastructure of library automation from which online library services are delivered. CENTRA, Central Michigan University Libraries' online catalog, represents a collection of over 850,000 volumes and 5,400 serial titles. It is available to EDP students and faculty through dial-up access and the Internet. The OCLS program is a full-service circulation point for off-campus borrowing. Also available for direct online searching and downloading are citations and abstracts from bibliographic databases such as ERIC, Expanded Academic Index, and Business Index. Other databases like Health Plan will be added in the future. These core, online services establish a basis for the introduction of a new mix of online services, such as electronic reference services via e-mail, interactive television instruction, and computer-mediated instruction.

Rapidly developing telecommunications and computing technology and the extraordinary development of the Internet and its library-related applications make the planning of online services daunting. Nevertheless, it is in this area where competition will be intense and librarians will be continually challenged to turn new information technologies into library services. Library programs that make online services easy to use, efficient, and, at the same time, flexible (with regard to the varying needs and capacities of students), will be invaluable for distance-education programs. The planning and decision making involved in the purchase of information technology to support these services is complex; among the many factors to consider are potential modes of access that students have to computer hardware, software, and telecommunications packages. Expectations of the services will mirror the student's level of expertise and access, and this level will range from the novice and unequipped at one end to the sophisticate at the other. The provision of Internet, subsidized dial-up, and toll-free access will have to be considered. The strategy of OCLS at Central Michigan University is to address the spectrum of user needs, i.e., to support the novice through the sophisticate. OCLS offers direct, unmediated online access to an electronic catalog and electronic bibliographic databases. A library Gopher server that will provide additional useful institutional information to students is also in the planning stage and will provide many more sources of information.

The expansion of online library services for the off-campus student involves the cost issue of computer support for user assistance and of technical support for systems administration. The technology of access is a service enhancement only if it is manageable by the patrons. New and innovative technology will likely require even greater end user support. Online bibliographic and full-text databases will proliferate and so will the hardware and software required to make them available. Gopher servers are another area where the potential for online service is enormous. A Gopher server can function in a very ambitious capacity as a comprehensive institutional information resource that offers access to local databases and information systems and to specialized electronic references sources, as well as one that points researchers to resources beyond the institution. However, a Gopher server can also be set up for more limited and specific services. World Wide Web servers can perform in a similar capacity as the Gopher server and add the multimedia dimension.

While standardization in computing and telecommunications is an ideal toward which progress is being made, systems differ in protocols and command language. The cost of user training and instruction must be factored into planning for the delivery of new online services. Technical support for systems administration also becomes increasingly complex. Systems have to be backed up. The backups need to be inventoried. Print jobs need to be managed along with the scheduling and running of batch jobs. File structure and hierarchy needs to be documented. User security must be carefully monitored—users will be continuously added and dropped from the systems. System upgrades need to be planned so as to cause users the least disruption due to downtime. Computer documentation itself must be organized and maintained. New systems and system upgrades also mean additional staff training.

Online information technology makes innovative service initiatives possible. However, the cost is considerable, not just in hardware and software, which are the most obvious expense, but in personnel, training, and support costs as well.

DOCUMENT DELIVERY

The existing technical capacities to digitize, store, and transmit information makes document delivery one of the most important, if not the most important, of future library services. Digitalization, not only of textual information but of sound and visual images, radically transforms both the physical and sociological conditions for teaching and learning by making the fruits of learning, i.e., knowledge, information, and intellectual creation, completely and immediately portable, exchangeable, and archivable. The role and place of the technology of information access takes on an increasingly important role in library planning and decision making.

The development of Standardized General Markup Language (SGML) means that electronic documents can be coded so as to permit a level of analysis and manipulation that provides an unparalleled level of bibliographic control at the document level. SGML functions as a kind of computerized metalanguage, a language, if you will, which describes in a highly formal and standardized way the structure of documents. As a powerful standard, SGML will provide "an essential service by making possible the exchange of information at any level of complexity between software, hardware, storage, and presentation systems" (Goldfarb 1990: x). SGML means a greater standardization of information packaging and manipulation, and hence even more portability and transferability. It will be necessary for librarians to become familiar with and knowledgeable about SGML just as they have with MARC.

The development of the Internet is opening many different kinds of opportunities for access to the contents of the world's great archives, libraries, and information databanks. The commercial sector is also creating new services like OCLC's FirstSearch and CARL's Uncover, which offer students at all locations an even greater number of options for delivery of documents in a timely fashion.

For off-campus library programs, these developments are particularly propitious and exciting since they mean that students in distant and remote locations can have timely access to all kinds of information. Off-campus library programs can, in effect, coordinate and facilitate document delivery technologies and can be instrumental in training patrons in the use of information technology. The transferring and downloading of files over the Internet, including multimedia files, will become an increasingly common way of gaining access to information. The technical challenge that off-campus library service programs face in document delivery is both the immediate problem of placing needed documents in the hands of students in a rapid, timely fashion and the more long-range problem of building a current system in a way that will allow its technical sophistication to evolve. It will be more cost-effective to "grow" systems, that is to purchase equipment configurations that have the potential to be added to, upgraded, and developed in an incremental fashion, than to replace old systems with new ones. While the technology for the delivery of information is enormously sophisticated, the capacities at the user end differ considerably in terms of the kinds of equipment available, the technical conditions of the local telecommunications infrastructure, and the level of computing sophistication.

CMU's Program

Central Michigan University's OCLS program has been a pioneer in document delivery. In the 1993–1994 fiscal year, the document delivery office processed over 110,000 document requests for specific items. Off-campus students and faculty can access the main campus libraries' collection when they have specific items to request, such as books, journals, or government documents. They do so by using a toll-free telephone number and by faxing or e-mailing requests via the Internet to the document delivery service based on the main campus. Up to fifteen items can be requested for each week a student is enrolled in a single class.

Books are loaned for one month and are sent via United Parcel or first-class mail to the requestor. CMU has an integrated online library system, using NOTIS software. OCLS is a full-service circulation point for off-campus borrowing. If they choose, EDP students and faculty can search CMU's entire book and serial title collections through CENTRA. This prerequest search using a personal computer and modem often helps the user determine if the CMU Library has the material they plan to request.

Copies of journal articles are the most frequently requested item type. These are reproduced free of charge and sent to the requestor. For collection development purposes, records are kept for materials' fill rates for books and journal articles. For each request received, a "Materials Request Form" is generated and returned to the requestor reporting the results of the inquiry by "action" categories. The reason(s) for failing to supply the needed material(s) are recorded. If 50 percent or less of the items requested can be supplied, the student is immediately contacted by telephone and given the report so that he or she can make alternative requests.

When made, the requests are entered into the unit's computerized database system. The system is a Unix-based IBM RISC System/6000 using AIX and Informix software to operate the system and manage the data. Requests for library materials are processed on a 24-hour turnaround basis from the time they are received until the time they leave the document delivery office. Timely delivery of documents is one of the major keys to the success of the program.

OCLS's document delivery program serves as a model to provide a general perspective for the kind of planning and decision making that applies to making document delivery an important, indeed core, library service. A number of issues related to planning emerge here. With the implementation of the IBM RISC/6000, an eight-year-old ALTOS system was replaced. From a planning perspective the purchase of the RISC/6000 provides a continuity of current services. At the same time, it puts into place an important infrastructure component for the future delivery of digitized information across the Internet, including full-text document delivery from sources like OCLC's FirstSearch and CARL's Uncover as well as access to the full-text databases on CD-ROM that reside at the host institution. The dramatic reduction in the costs of CD-ROM disk-mastering technology make it possible for libraries to acquire specialized full-text databases and make them available to their publics. The purchase of the RISC/6000 system by OCLS also created a need for programming support personnel. This need was not immediately realized at the time of purchase. This is an example of the personnel factor affecting both cost and service. New systems often require people to have hands-on experience in order to comprehend what technical staffing levels will be necessary to explore the new functionality. A full-time staff programmer position was created in order to provide the necessary programming and technical assistance, when it became apparent that additional technical expertise would be needed in order to obtain full functionality from the new system.

Again, an important but difficult issue in planning and decision making is with creating a technical infrastructure that enables the library to provide both a continuity in its services to the public and yet introduce innovative services that take full advantage of technological developments. To the extent that managers can plan so that the services of programs grow and incrementally develop, rather than having to make hasty qualitative leaps into new areas, the benefits of innovation will be more immediately obvious, easier to sell, and less costly.

CONCLUSION

Innovative off-campus library services are a key to the success of distance education. Behind the new information services that are transforming education and making distance education a growth industry in the educational marketplace is an increasingly complex and costly technical infrastructure. The library automation market-place, driven as it is by complex technical innovation, is highly competitive and volatile. And so, while off-campus library managers and administrators must focus on innovative information service to the public, it must be remembered that technical services provide the underlying support for the viability of such programs. Furthermore, adequate technical services support requires near continuous planning in order to cope with the factors of rapid change, the pressures of innovation, and the increasing complexity of computing.

REFERENCES

Goldfarb, Charles F. 1990. *The SGML Handbook.* Oxford: Clarendon Press.
Goodyear, Mary Lou, and Jane Dodd. 1994. "From the Library of Record to the Library as Gateway: An Analysis of Three Electronic Table-of-Contents Services." *Library Acquisitions: Practice and Theory* 18: 253–264.
Huber, Peter. 1994. "Bye-Bye, Big Brother." *National Review* (August 15): 48–50.
Jacobson, Robert L. 1994. "Information Technology: The Coming Revolution." *Chronicle of Higher Education* (April 27): A26–A29.
McCabe, Gerard B. 1986. "Library Service for Off-Campus Institutions." In *The Off-Campus Library Services Conference Proceedings,* ed. Barton Lessin. Mt. Pleasant, Mich.: Central Michigan University Press, pp. 172–189.
Perelman, Lewis J. 1992. *Schools Out: Hyperlearning, the New Technology, and the End of Education.* New York: William Morrow and Co.

7

Utilization of Developing Technologies for Cataloging

Susan E. Ketcham

In cataloging departments across the country, many librarians are facing a critical decision—is the utilization of CD-ROMs (CDs) and the Internet to find MARC records as part of the day-to-day operation feasible?

Are catalogers already taking advantage of this new technology? If not, why not? What impact, if any, does this technology have on workload? Can it be used by technical services librarians to help perform their work more efficiently?

To answer these and other questions related to the utilization of developing technologies, a survey was developed and mailed to 204 libraries. The participating libraries were categorized by holdings: under 100,000 volumes, 100,000–499,000 volumes, 500,000–999,000 volumes, and over one million volumes; and by professional cataloger staff size: less than 1,[1] 1–2, 3–5, 6–9, and 10 or more. In all, 108 surveys were returned for a 53 percent response rate.

BIBLIOGRAPHIC UTILITIES

Before determining whether catalogers are using "new" technology, it is interesting to ascertain whether they are using "old" technology. When asked whether they currently use a bibliographic utility such as Online Computer Library Center (OCLC) for cataloging, 96 percent reported that they do. Not surprisingly, an overwhelming majority (84 percent) of those catalogers who responded yes to the above question, listed OCLC as their bibliographic utility. Other bibliographic utilities named were: Western Library Network (WLN) (6 percent), Bibliofile (2 percent), Research Library Information Network (RLIN) (2 percent) and Southeastern Library Network (SOLINET) (1 percent). Seven percent of the respondents did not identify a bibliographic utility. Bibliographic utilities are chiefly used by those libraries that fall into the 100,000–499,000 volumes group and by those libraries with at least six professional staff members.

The main alternative source of cataloging information used by catalogers is the National Union Catalog (NUC), though several did say they use the Internet.

CD SYSTEMS

There are several CD-ROM cataloging support systems available today, including Bibliofile, CAT CD450, CDMARC Names, CDMARC Subjects, Precision One, and SuperCat. Some of the CD-ROM software can be used in combination with a bibliographic utility or they can stand on their own. Knowing what some of the advantages of each system are may make the decision to use one or another easier.

Bibliofile contains the Library of Congress Machine Readable Cataloging (LC MARC) database plus extensive indexes. It allows for copying to floppy or hard disks, enabling the creation of a locally maintainable database. Records may be modified, and there are multiple search access points. Barcode readers can be attached for direct input of circulation information. Updates are monthly.

OCLC's CAT CD450 combines offline cataloging with batch processing. It does not replace the online connection and current online catalog, but it can stand on its own. CAT CD450 is not compatible with other software, and a library must be an OCLC subscriber to purchase it. Full-record editing and cataloging tasks, such as catalog cards, labels, and exporting can be done offline. Catalog cards can be produced locally. Bibliographic records can be batch exported in OCLC-MARC format to a local system. CAT CD450 consists of seven cataloging collections: recent books cataloging collection, older books and most-used nonbook collection, law cataloging collection, medical cataloging collection, music cataloging collection, Hispanic cataloging collection, and LC authorities collection.

The LC Authorities Collection is the complete file of the Library of Congress Name and Subject Authority records. Its source is the OCLC Online Union Catalog. The CDs are updated quarterly and are cumulative. They may be purchased as a set or separately.

Precision One contains LC MARC records. The titles are prechosen and are representative of the titles most frequently held by school and public libraries. The CDs are updated monthly.

SuperCat contains the LC MARC Record database of English bibliographic records (foreign records on an additional disc is optional). It can stand alone as an ongoing cataloging workstation or as a retrospective conversion utility with the LC MARC records database as a source of cataloging records.

The most important advantage of CD-ROM catalog systems is that "the Library of Congress (LC) file of the MARC (Machine Readable Cataloging) bibliographic records forms the base for all the compact disc (CD) cataloging support systems currently being marketed" (Upham 1989: 146). Therefore, catalogers can continue to add records to their local online database or card catalog that meet the same national cataloging standards as the online bibliographic utilities.

Some available software, such as CAT CD450 and SuperCat, can emulate online bibliographic utility functions; for example, original cataloging, editing records, preparing statistical reports, and printing cards, labels, and pockets. Other software is helpful with retrospective conversion projects. All of the CD-ROM systems that have been mentioned can be used for retrospective conversion. Several respondents cited this as the reason their CD-ROM software was purchased.

CD-ROM cataloging support systems have the same advantages of CD-ROM technology in general, large memory storage capacity on one disc and multiple search access points. A good illustration of this is *The Cataloger's Desktop,* which is available from the Library of Congress. On one disc can be found all the following: Library of Congress Rule Interpretations, Subject Cataloging Manual: Subject Headings, Subject Cataloging Manual: Classification, USMARC Concise Formats, USMARC Authority Format, plus all of the USMARC Code Lists.

When asked if they use their bibliographic utility in conjunction with a CD-ROM cataloging system for cataloging new material or retrospective conversion projects, 87 percent of the respondents said they did not. They relied on their bibliographic utilities to perform standard cataloging functions. Of those who do, the CAT CD450 or the CDMARC Names and CDMARC Subjects are the most popular systems. In addition, the majority of those who currently use a CD-ROM system, do so for cataloging both current materials and retrospective conversion. Only six respondents (6 percent) use it for card and label production, while the greater number use their bibliographic utility. (An added sidenote: more than half of the respondents do not use the cataloging microenhancer software.)

For what reasons are libraries not using these systems? While there were several libraries that cited their workloads or their staffs as too small to warrant the expenditure, the two most common reasons were "too expensive" and "not necessary." While a prohibitive cost factor may have been true when the cataloging CD-ROM products were first on the market, that is not the case today. According to Dolly Chao, CD-ROM software has some of the same one-time costs, such as hardware purchase (unless leased), telecommunications installation charges, and training; in addition, recurring costs that are associated with both a bibliographic utility or a CD-ROM–based cataloging system include hardware maintenance, software maintenance and updates, and telecommunications charges (1989: 50).

While the question of necessity will, of course, be different for each situation, CD-ROMs have proven themselves to be useful to catalogers in several ways: retrospective projects, for both general and special projects; doing cataloging work offline; and exporting records to a local system.

Nearly half of the cataloging departments have approximately 2–4 terminals for cataloging purposes. As one might suspect, those libraries with professional staffs of 10 or more and with collections in excess of one million volumes, which generally presuppose larger budgets, fell into the 5+ terminals category.

Most of the respondents using a CD-ROM product for cataloging (11 percent) were not trained by the CD-ROM software company, but those who were trained by the company representative felt the training overall was adequate. The majority of professionals rated their computer skills as competent prior to the purchase of CD-ROM software.

Those who use CD-ROM software felt that it did ease the departments' workload, although a small number felt that it had no impact on the workload at all. Fourteen out of the 16 respondents who use CD-ROM software said they would recommend the CD-ROM systems they were using to other librarians.

THE INTERNET

What is the Internet? The Internet is a "network of networks"—a backbone that connects smaller networks such as BITNET and enables these networks to communicate with each other by means of a standard language or "protocol" (Warren-Wenk, 1994).

The benefits to a catalog librarian of accessing remote catalogs through the Internet include the opportunity to verify a citation or to find an appropriate subject heading or to see how someone else classified a particular item.

For a catalog librarian, these two fundamental applications on the Internet are a benefit:

1. Remote log-in—telnet/gophers/mosaic—accessing national and international OPACS (Online Public Access Computer Systems), databases, and online informational services.
2. File transfer protocol (ftp)—the transfer of documents, software, or images.

While almost all respondents (96 percent) said they were familiar with Internet, the percentage dropped to 89 percent for those with access to Internet and to 69 percent for those with access from their terminals. For those without access from their terminals, either the reference department or the campus computer center was the nearest access point. Several respondents said they would be getting access, and in some cases direct access, in the near future.

Thirty-seven percent of the Internet users received training for the Internet in their library. Twenty-five percent of Internet users got training from the campus computer center, and 19 percent attended a library workshop for instruction.

Thirty-seven percent of Internet users are self-taught. For 23 respondents, their training was a combination of two or more kinds of training. All but one had a combination of in-house (from colleagues) and self-taught instruction. Respondents were equally split between campus computer center and library workshop sessions as an additional means of Internet instruction.

When asked how they would rate their Internet skills, 20 percent of responders said poor, 55 percent said fair, and 8 percent said very good. Since 75 percent of the respondents rate their Internet user skills as poor to fair, additional training would appear to be needed. Two possible sources of training sessions are library schools and library conferences. Occasionally, there can also be an online Internet user instruction course. These are usually posted on discussion groups. In-service Internet workshops taught by personnel from the on-campus computer center can easily be geared toward various skill levels and can be repeated more frequently throughout the academic year. One source of training that should not be overlooked is in-house training, which makes use of colleagues' training, learned skills, and tricks.

When asked if they have subscribed to Autocat (a library cataloging and authorities online discussion group), 64 percent said they did. Of that group, 61 percent indicated they used it to request help with a problem, 64 percent used it to reply to a problem, and 88 percent just read messages.

Besides accessing Autocat, other cataloging uses cited for the Internet included: browsing through remote card catalogs, accessing the Library of Congress, sending electronic mail (e-mail) to cataloging colleagues, accessing online discussion groups other than Autocat and ftp/telnet/gopher.

CONCLUSION

CD-ROM cataloging software products are slowly garnering the attention of catalogers from small, medium, and large academic libraries. Several of the respondents (6 percent) indicated that they had a system under consideration. The software has already proven to be advantageous to libraries who are engaging in short-term or long-term retrospective conversion projects. It can also work with or independently of a bibliographic utility.

Between cataloging (current materials/retrospective conversion) and reference work, cataloging staffs may be a bit overwhelmed by their present workload. Particularly affected are those cataloging in small- to medium-sized libraries where the prospect of additional staff may be unlikely.

As a cataloger and/or department manager, there are several benefits one needs to think about when considering utilization of a CD-ROM software product or the Internet. The first step is to review the department's current workflows. Some may be rethought, revised, and improved with the application of a CD-ROM product. Take, for example, processing time: how long can an item remain in the department before it is made available for patron use? By using a CD-ROM product such as CAT CD450 or SuperCat, it is possible to catalog, export the record to a local system (or to produce catalog cards locally), and make labels. This would expedite the processing of materials and make them available for patron use in relatively short periods of time.

Another area of concern that can be addressed by CD-ROM cataloging products is cost. Since no libraries have the luxury of an unlimited budget, it is important for each department to do the best it can with what it is allotted to spend. One of the best features of CD-ROM software is the ability to do work offline. Whether offline work is limited to just searching out MARC records by using products like CDMARC Names, CDMARC Subjects, or Precision One or to using a bibliographic utility with such software as Bibliofile, CAT CD450, or Supercat, it is possible to lower cataloging costs. In addition, by doing work offline, searching does not have to be limited to prime-time hours, which is an added cost.

There are two potential disadvantages to using CD-ROM cataloging software: records are not automatically entered on the bibliographic utility and the frequency of updates vary.

Given the variety of CD-ROM cataloging software that is accessible today, catalogers need to take the time to investigate what products might meet their libraries' needs.

According to Gillian McCombs, technical services librarians have remained largely uninvolved with the Internet, and it remains essentially unexplored as a technical resource (1993: 169). The results of this survey, however, show a large number of respondents (89 percent) who are actively using the Internet. This would seem to indicate that the trend McCombs suggests is being reversed. Among the Internet resources presently being used by catalogers are: OCLC's web site, LOCIS (Library of Congress Information System), LC's web site, and the ALA (American Library Association) gopher/telnet site.

One serious disadvantage to keep in mind when using the Internet is the possibility of a broken network connection. If there are problems with either the host computer or with the local communications lines, or problems with the Internet service provider (also called the carrier), no e-mail can be delivered.

Several of the respondents stated that they were unfamiliar with the Autocat online discussion group (6 percent) or the Internet (4 percent), because they had not yet had time to look into them. Whether the cataloging department consists of one professional staff member or many, it is important to take the time to explore, research, and to experiment on the Internet. It is the best way to discover what is new, what is on the horizon, and what other libraries are doing with the current technology. More importantly, it is the means by which catalog librarians may discover how they may best utilize these technologies in their libraries.

NOTE

1. Two libraries did not have a full-time cataloger.

REFERENCES

Chao, Dolly. 1989. "Cost Comparisons Between Bibliographic Utilities and CD-ROM–based Cataloging Systems." *Library Hi Tech* 7: 49–51.

Fiste, David A. 1993. "Bibliographic Services of the Future." *Technical Services Quarterly* 10: 27–43.

McCombs, Gillian. 1993. "The Internet and Technical Services: A Point Break Approach." *Library Resources and Technical Services* 38: 169–177.

Upham, Lois N. 1989. "Cataloging Outside the Network." In *Operations Handbook for the Small Academic Library*, ed. Gerard B. McCabe. Westport, Conn.: Greenwood Press, pp. 145–151.

Warren-Wenk, P. 1994. "Moving Toward Internet Literacy on the University Campus." In *The Internet Library: Case Studies of Library Internet Management and Use*, ed. Julie Still. Westport, Conn.: Mecklermedia, pp. 127–165.

8

Managing the Use of Automated Bibliographic Databases in the Cataloging Department

Christine E. Thompson

The introduction of automated bibliographic databases, such as Online Computer Library Center (OCLC), Research Libraries Information Network (RLIN), UTLAS International (now CATSS), and Western Libraries Network (WLN), revolutionized the process of cataloging and created an entirely different approach to the management of cataloging. Workflows changed dramatically in an effort to take advantage of the benefits of using computerized cataloging. Staffing requirements and levels of responsibilities were also changed dramatically in order to allow catalogers more time for original cataloging and research and to allow support staff a greater sense of accomplishment and creativity in their positions.

The additional sources for automated cataloging that are more cost-efficient for smaller libraries that cannot afford the major bibliographic utilities may be of questionable value for larger research libraries. CDMARC Bibliographic allows a cataloger to access the Library of Congress catalog via CD-ROM. Commercial companies can supply libraries with other CD-ROM products, such as Bibliofile from Bro-Dart. Approval vendors like Blackwell North America send acquisitions librarians a disk or tape, which is a compilation of bibliographic records corresponding to the approval titles sent to the library as a part of the approval plan profile.

Large academic libraries will need to consider carefully the usefulness of the above-mentioned catalog record sources before starting to use them in conjunction with their holdings. For a community whose researchers range from a postdoctoral professor requiring publications in several languages to a beginning freshman writing an English class essay, the catalog department head must be aware of these demographics in order to meet as many research needs as possible, while taking into consideration time, staff, and cost. A high level of quality control and subject specialization must be built into the bibliographic database, which is the research library catalog.

As a result of this technological activity, cataloging department heads must learn how to manage and control automated cataloging tools and resources. If this control is not applied and proper management not engaged in, the inevitable result will be ever-increasing costs. The increasing costs of technical services, and in particular cataloging, have brought some academic cataloging departments to a point of financial exigency, which has prompted library administrators to look closely at the cataloging operation (Hirshon 1994: 17). The catalog department head has an obligation to use this technology wisely and cost-effectively in order to stay in control of the process of catalog production and maintenance, or they will see that process transferred to outside providers.

COST-CONTAINMENT ISSUES

Cost containment is a high priority in any library, especially today when budgets are shrinking while costs for materials and processing of those materials are growing rapidly. Many research libraries are finding it necessary to reduce collection development costs by canceling serial subscriptions and allocating less monies to monographic acquisitions. In order to stretch shrinking budgets further and possibly transfer money back into the acquisition of materials, libraries are beginning to explore the avenues for cost containment in the technical services area. Before the cataloging manager can effectively evaluate methods for reductions in costs, however, a cost study of the current operation must be done. It is necessary to know how much is spent currently to catalog and process materials before decisions can be made concerning where and how to reduce or contain those expenditures.

In large academic and research libraries, one of the most significant expenditures is automation. These costs must be accounted for when determining overall operating costs. The equipment used for the processing of materials and the costs for maintaining this equipment have been decreasing recently due to the reduction in costs for computers, but equipment and maintenance are still expensive. In addition to the equipment, the costs levied by the bibliographic utilities for copy cataloging as well as the costs and/or cost reductions for original cataloging must be identified. Telecommunications costs must be factored into any study of automated cataloging operations expenses.

Cost studies can be simple or elaborate, depending on the amount of time and detail used for the analysis. A simple approach is to divide the annual operating costs for the department by the annual cataloging production, determining a quick-and-dirty estimate of the average cost of cataloging one item.

Much better costing methods exist in the literature of technical services and should be consulted before embarking on this project. The Technical Services Costs Committee of the Association for Library Collections and Technical Services (ALCTS) has published an easy-to-use, accurate guide to costing (1991: 49–52).

Another excellent guide for costing methods can be found in Morris's article (1992: 79–95) relating a study done at Iowa State University in Ames. The formula outlined in the article is detailed but extremely accurate in its results. Based on the separate tasks involved in performing each technical service function and the amount of time required to perform each task, Morris's method can yield, highly accurate and scientific calculations for the exact costs of acquiring and cataloging an item.

One of the critical managerial decisions concerning cost containment and automated cataloging systems involves deciding how to use the machine resources effectively. One of the most expensive tools used for cataloging is the bibliographic utility. There are varying charges that include membership dues as well as system usage for cataloging tasks. Some utilities give credits to libraries for contributions to the system and thus offset those charges. The catalog department manager needs to be aware of both charges and credits generated by his or her department since he or she is responsible for providing good catalog copy within an automated services budget. Currently, only an item-by-item accounting of the monthly billing will yield this information. However, OCLC is testing a cataloging service concept that would set a single monthly subscription price for a library's cataloging needs and, if successful, would eliminate the need for item-by-item accounting (Thompson 1994: 1).

Many libraries routinely enhance and upgrade records found in the bibliographic databases both as a professional service and, if allowed, in order to receive the price breaks for providing this information. By making these enhancements, catalogers are providing quality cataloging for both their own library patrons and other catalogers using the database.

Some research libraries use one set of vendor tapes to download records directly onto their local databases and then another set to send information on their holdings to the bibliographic utilities. For a small fee, the utilities will then use the tapes to attach each library's holdings to the utility's online bibliographic records. This method eliminates some of the costs of searching for and updating utility records. Many federal document depository libraries use tape records from vendors, such as MARCive, to download bibliographic information onto the library's online catalog. The library can then purchase a tape from MARCive, which can be sent to a bibliographic utility such as OCLC. The utility will then attach the library's holdings code to the appropriate record for interlibrary loan purposes. OCLC released another vendor tape-load service, called PromptCat, in 1995.

Approval plan vendors who join PromptCat will provide OCLC with a list of the approval plan items being sent to a particular library. OCLC will provide the appropriate record, download it electronically to the library's database, and attach the library's holdings to the downloaded record.

Only time and experience with vendor tape-load and OCLC services will provide definitive answers as to the desirability of these vendor databases to the large academic library. Some vendors cannot provide sufficient cataloging information to comply with the quality standards needed by larger research libraries, while other vendors will provide the quality of cataloging specified by an individual library through profiling. Additionally, some vendors will provide both authority records and MARC-based bibliographic records while others have no authority control and do not use bibliographic records compatible with MARC-based systems. Most importantly, before adopting any of these cost-containment measures, the department head must assess costs and effects on both cataloging quality and workflow.

Cooperative cataloging was from the beginning one of the enormous benefits of automated cataloging. Through the use of the bibliographic utilities and other bibliographic databases like Bibliofile, cataloging records become available to the local library for downloading and editing. However, like almost everything else in automation, this is both a help and a hindrance to the catalog department manager. The manager must be careful that the appropriate balance between not checking anything (and therefore sacrificing quality) and checking everything (and therefore sacrificing time and money savings) is maintained.

According to James Rush (1994: 12), too many catalog departments actually reinvent the bibliographic record with each item being cataloged. He found that the ten most popular bibliographic records in OCLC were updated by individual libraries over 1,000 times per record. Assuming that many of these changes were cosmetic in an effort to achieve the "perfect" record, updating all automated bibliographic records could be very expensive and perhaps not necessary. The amount of time spent in carefully checking all information in the record may far outweigh the benefits that might be gained through this practice. However, the assumption that extensive editing is not necessary and only adds to the costs of cataloging cannot automatically be made in all libraries. Attention to the needs of the user of the research library may dictate that catalog records be edited and enhanced (to provide better access and information for research) more frequently than the catalog records for the smaller library. In either type of library, the automatic perusal of every record for catching all errors is usually not necessary and very costly.

The only way the cataloger can assess the costs and benefits of extensive editing is to study thoroughly the needs of the library patrons. The catalog manager must be aware of the unique needs of the individual library patron to be able to make an informed judgment as to when and where it is essential to edit records to conform to local practices and policies. The large research library may find an extensive amount of enhancing, editing, and updating of records is essential, if the catalog is to serve as an effective research tool for all patrons. Large academic libraries are now experimenting with contents listings for almost all their collections and with back-of-the-book indexes, in an effort to provide more access to the information found within the item. In many cases, the omission of optional elements of descriptive information requires that an individual library update the record to include the missing data. Cost-effectiveness considerations will always lead the department head to decide that editing of records for the general good of the catalog and the individual library are to be encouraged, while editing simply to achieve a "perfect" record is to be discouraged.

In any automated catalog system, searching and editing costs should be factors in cost containment. Whereas the bibliographic utilities have charges attached to searching for, editing, and downloading an appropriate record into the local catalog, the CD-ROM databases bought from commercial vendors will not carry these costs. However, trade-offs may need to be made. The CD-ROM may have fewer records matching the needs of the library, which creates a need for more in-house original cataloging. It may also be necessary to cope with reduced automated resource sharing capabilities through interlibrary loan due to the lack of a connection to a bibliographic utility's interlibrary loan union listing file. These trade-offs are not feasible for the large research libraries, who must depend on each other for interlibrary loan support for their scholars and for copy cataloging of a major percentage of their new acquisitions. Without access to interlibrary loan, libraries would never be capable of supplying all the information needed by their patrons and, without access to a large bibliographic database for cataloging purposes, large libraries would not be able to sustain the enormous costs of original cataloging. However, since no one source is capable of providing access to all the information needed by a large research library, there is a blending of bibliographic utilities, bibliographic CD-ROM software for cataloging, tape-loads, and other electronic sources for finding cataloging information and attaching holdings to interlibrary loan databases.

WORKFLOW CHANGES AND CONSIDERATIONS

Far too often, in some automated cataloging operations, paper workforms are still passed from one catalog station to another or from the acquisitions department to the catalog department. A workflow that allows an automated record to be used by each person in the process is much more cost-effective and efficient. Many libraries have changed their automated cataloging procedures to use the system more effectively and to reduce the incidence of paperwork related to acquiring and cataloging materials. In many research libraries, searching for and downloading an appropriate record for cataloging is done at the "point of order" in the acquisitions process. Order information is attached to an appropriate bibliographic record or, if a record is not found, to a provisional record provided by acquisitions personnel. Any subsequent changes made by the appropriate people in the catalog department are made online in the local system. Only original cataloging is done online through the utility. No paper copies are needed and, except for original cataloging, no further searching or editing is done through the bibliographic utility.

Commercial vendor tapes of bibliographic records have not always changed the way in which research library cataloging departments handle materials, primarily due to the need for stringent quality control. When federal depository libraries purchase MARCive tapes of government publications, some download the tape information, send the materials to the documents staff for processing, and catalog the material from both the processing information and the tape information. Other depository libraries use the MARCive information for the download, but route all materials through the catalog department, for final cataloging and processing.

Several approval book plan jobbers, such as Blackwell North America, provide tapes or disks of records corresponding to their approval book shipments to libraries. OCLC's PromptCat also provides approval book records to libraries. Catalog managers must make several decisions in advance concerning the usage of these record sources to ensure that the library is using them effectively and that quality is maintained. As a result, some catalog departments have changed workflows and job responsibilities for staff.

Some large research libraries have defined certain types of records as acceptable quality and items with these designated records are cataloged at the point of acquisitions check-in and order confirmation. For example, a record that is cataloged by the Library of Congress, using the most recent cataloging rules and full-level descriptive entries, would be cataloged in acquisitions and the item would not be sent to cataloging. In this workflow scenario, all decisions concerning authority work, cross-references, and the definition of a quality record must be made before the items arrive in the library.

Some research libraries will choose to let the problems with authority control be caught by a quality-control unit after the item has been cataloged. Other libraries will not be able to perform quality control at the end of the cataloging process and will find that it is necessary to maintain the original workflow, requiring all items to be cataloged in the catalog department. Each library must decide which scenario provides the desired balance of efficiency of workflow and effective quality control.

The demise of many of the paper files found in the catalog department precipitated a crisis in shelf listing practices in those research libraries that discontinued card shelf listing. Granted, the call number search can be utilized as a shelf list checkpoint and author numbers can be aligned properly through this checkpoint; but, in many cases, the local system does not allow for recording the other shelf list information commonly found on the card file. As a result, catalog department heads have to ascertain what can be recorded on the local system, where it can be recorded, and if the information is essential enough for the library to warrant recording. Of equal import is the question of the adequacy of an automated system that will not accommodate information on individual items previously kept on the shelf list cards.

QUALITY, QUANTITY, AND OTHER CATALOG MANAGEMENT PRIORITIES

Quality control is of primary concern to the catalog manager. Adherence to standards, such as Anglo-American cataloging rules and machine-readable bibliographic input standards, are required when inputting any data into an international bibliographic database, such as OCLC. Local automated systems also require standards for database quality if the system is to be usable and consistent. In a large research library, these standards become very important in order to blend the varying types of materials found in the research library and the varying levels of researchers using the collection. At the same time, the department head must determine the level, of quality control to apply and how to achieve the desired quality with a minimum of workflow disruption and production slowdowns. The volume of materials coming through the large library catalog department does not regularly permit exacting checking of every record, unless the library is willing to fund correspondingly large staffing levels. In today's tightening budgets, a large staff for cataloging purposes is neither realistic nor feasible. Therefore, other measures of achieving quality catalogs are necessary.

Many catalog departments use a system of quality control that may involve a senior cataloger proofing and evaluating junior catalogers as a part of the routine. This method is effective for catching errors and determining situations where individual retraining or revision of the training program is needed; but it is very costly in terms of staff time and reduced production levels. Some libraries have a system of periodic review of staff work in order to maintain quality and accuracy through correction and retraining when necessary. This alleviates the problems of costly staff time and production levels, but it is less effective for catching errors than the other method, which checks every record.

Still others have established a routine of error checks within a database maintenance unit, which oversees the quality of the bibliographic records in the library's catalog. This method reduces the costs of staff time and production levels and is very effective for trapping errors, but it does not address the need for individual retraining since no individuals are identified. Also, this method may not be possible for some libraries due to the lack of cataloging-error trapping and reporting available on the library's system.

When choosing a method of quality control, the catalog manager must first determine realistically the level of precision needed to achieve the desired level of catalog accuracy. After determining a realistic level of accuracy, the manager must then determine the method that is the most effective while being the least costly in terms of staff time and production levels. In summary, each method has advantages and disadvantages and the catalog manager must evaluate each one according to the individual library's staff, equipment, and time.

Some catalog departments specify critical errors and noncritical errors and exercise levels of quality control based on these criteria. A noncritical error is an error that does not affect access to the bibliographic record. This error would be caught and corrected but would not be considered serious enough to warrant retraining for the individual committing the error. A critical error would be an error that seriously violates cataloging standards or renders the record inaccessible. This error would not only be corrected but would be considered reason for the cataloger to be retrained in the area where the error was committed. If more than one cataloger is committing the same critical error, a revision of the training program may be desirable. In any case and by whatever means the department proposes to establish a quality-control mechanism, it is essential to the success of the machine catalog that quality control be established.

STAFFING LEVELS FOR EFFICIENCY AND EFFECTIVE USE OF PERSONNEL

Computerization has created a problem when trying to determine paraprofessional and professional duties. Copy cataloging by paraprofessionals has been hailed as the future of the catalog department and the harbinger of the demise of the professional cataloger (Intner 1993: 6). We have learned since the decade of the 1980s that the truth lies somewhere on the continuum between the two extremes.

The catalog manager must find the appropriate division of duties for the department's staff. Paraprofessional staff, like professional librarians, need to feel a sense of accomplishment and pride in the work that they are assigned. Many of these staff persons have several years of experience in cataloging materials and need to be placed in a position that utilizes this experience and expertise. Copy cataloging can be challenging if the appropriate personnel are matched with the proper level of needed knowledge.

Professional catalogers in today's world need to be far more than original catalogers. The knowledge base for a cataloger now includes database management, personnel management, and research expertise. Intner defines four areas in which the professional cataloger must be knowledgeable: (1) standards, which include descriptive cataloging standards, machine cataloging standards, and media standards; (2) management; (3) research for planning and decision making; and (4) computing (1993: 8).

According to Allen Veaner, the professional librarian is responsible for programmatic decisions, which analyze and reshape the responsibilities of the future of librarianship and the library in which they work, while paraprofessional staffing is essential for the task management and job assignments of the library (1994: 393–396). Each of these staffing levels is necessary in automated cataloging and cannot be interchanged. The department head needs to have a clear understanding of what constitutes programmatic responsibilities and what constitutes task-management responsibilities. Once this understanding is achieved and defined, then clearer definitions of both professional and paraprofessional duties can be developed and put into place in the catalog department.

Using both Veaner's and Intner's descriptions of the skills and responsibilities of the library staff, the primary concerns of the cataloger are standards analysis and design, database management, original cataloging, and research for establishing policies and procedures; while the primary concerns of the paraprofessional are managing and performing the daily tasks necessary to carry out the policies and procedures established within the cataloging operation.

A "gray area" could exist when the responsibilities of the originial cataloger and the paraprofessional cataloger are not clearly defined in accordance with the skills and training necessary for the cataloging being performed. Before the catalog manager can set the needed definitions, however, careful study of the job descriptions and possible restrictions on types of tasks defined for the positions must be done. There may also be a careful consideration of the affected positions and the utilization of future new staff in terms of training and knowledge for the new job requirements.

A third level of staffing that is frequently not mentioned in the professional literature is the student assistant. Catalog departments rely on small cadres of student assistants to help with special projects, to do the shelf processing, and to do other tasks that are a normal part of any department within the library. When assigning student tasks the department manager should consider the training needs of the student assistant in relation to that student's future plans. In today's world the heavy reliance upon the computerization of cataloging operations can benefit many students in nonlibrary-related studies as well as provide training for the library or information science student. Effective use of this valuable human resource should also be a priority for the department head.

STAFF DEVELOPMENT AND TRAINING FOR BETTER PERFORMANCE

In today's automated cataloging departments, continual training and staff development is essential. This training and development can be obtained either through commercial avenues or through in-house training and development programs. A library's choice of commercial or in-house training may depend on the degree of relevance to the library's specific training needs and/or the cost of the training and its impact on the budget. Research libraries with large cataloging staffs frequently find that the expertise to supply in-house training exists and is more cost-effective than commercial training.

Several types of commercial training for automated cataloging can be utilized by a library; however, the most commonly used by the large library are those offered by the bibliographic networks. Network distributors for the bibliographic utilities will normally provide the initial training for the utility's cataloging system. These sessions are designed to train librarians who are new to the use of the utilities either through affiliation with a new member library or through recent entry into the catalog office of a member library. Some networks also offer for-a-fee training in other aspects of automation and/or automated cataloging. For example, the Southeastern Library Network (SOLINET) offers several training tracks, one of which is a cataloging track aimed at both professional and paraprofessional staff. Upon successful completion of the "track," the staff member receives a certificate of "track completion" (SOLINET 1995: 46). SOLINET also offers single sessions on many cataloging and noncataloging topics.

The use of these training opportunities by a large library may not be the most cost-effective method of training. If the library is a new member library and there is no resident expertise within the catalog department, then the initial training offered by the network is relevant and worth serious consideration. Most large academic libraries, however, are already members of one of the major networks and the training by the network is relevant only to the new employee, thus making in-house new cataloger training a more desirable choice. On the other hand, if the network training is being offered to demonstrate new techniques and/or system changes such as format integration, then the use of the network training is timely and convenient for developing the necessary expertise in the library.

In addition to the networks, independent consultants also provide cataloging training on a contractual basis for libraries. A department that has limited staff and training time might consider bringing one of these expert catalogers into the department for some period of time to provide updated information and training for the staff. In the case of training for a new program being initiated by the library, e.g., cooperative cataloging program, consultants brought into the library are a better choice than sending staff to the program offices for training. In many cases, almost all of the staff can be trained at one time by the consultant, making for faster and more accurate learning.

Assuming there is staff and time for in-house training, there are several options for providing this activity. Catalog departments need to compile a manual in support of on-the-job training programs for new catalogers, whether they are new to the profession or just new to the library. The amount of time spent to ensure a consistent and complete manual and developing the program is well spent, especially in light of a constantly changing automated environment. A well-developed program and a well-written manual will include a multitude of technical information necessary to perform the job effectively, but they will also include a multitude of necessary philosophical and library-specific information to show why the job is being performed. An excellent example of a training program is being developed by the ALCTS Cataloging and Classification Section (CCS) Committee on Education, Training, and Recruitment for Cataloging, and it can be found in *ALCTS Newsletter* (1994: 32–34).

The training manual should always include the policies and procedures manual of the department as a component. This one tool represents a major portion of the knowledge needed by any new staff member in the department. It will not replace but will enhance the myriad of automated system, bibliographic utility, CD-ROM product, and other documentation that is also needed in order to fully train and develop catalog department staff.

The professional literature has long upheld the concept of the cataloger spending brief periods of time in the public services area of the library in order to better understand the needs of the library patrons for access to and familiarity with the idiosyncracies of the automated catalog. Giving personnel the opportunity to work in other library departments will further develop their skills and knowledge. Spending brief periods of time within the acquisitions or the collections departments will allow staff to further understand the selection and acquisition process and, if some of the cataloging is done in acquisitions, will enhance understanding of the cataloging process at the point of order. Some time spent in the systems office of a library can also enhance the knowledge and skill of the catalog staff in the area of computerization.

SUMMARY

Cataloging should have two overriding priorities: the first of these is quality control for the catalog and all associated databases. Quality includes adherence to standards that may be dictated by the cataloging community or may be dictated by the machine on which cataloging is accomplished. The successful manager must be aware of those quality standards and know how to apply them with a minimum of workflow disruptions and production bottlenecks. The second priority for the cataloger is responding to the needs of the community for which the bibliographic database is provided: staff, faculty, and institution. The successful manager has a clear understanding of the needs of the library community and a clear definition of what constitutes acceptable levels of quality and usefulness for the database.

In a large research library, these priorities necessitate constant vigilance over the quality of the database and constant assessment of the usefulness of the database for all levels of research capabilities and needs. Today's catalog department head must meet the challenges by controlling and utilizing effectively the technology inherent in the modern catalog office.

REFERENCES

ALCTS CCS Committee on Education, Training, and Recruitment for Cataloging. 1994. "Essential Elements of Training Program for Entry-Level Professional Catalogers." *ALCTS Newsletter* 5(3): 32–34.

ALCTS Technical Services Costs Committee. 1991. "Guide to Cost Analysis of Acquisitions and Cataloging in Libraries." *ALCTS Newsletter* 2(5): 49–52.

Hirshon, Arnold. 1994. "The Lobster Quadrille: The Future of Technical Services in a Re-engineering World." In *The Future Is Now: The Changing Face of Technical Services.* Dublin, Ohio: Online Computer Library Center, Inc., pp. 14–20.

Intner, Sheila S. 1993. "The Re-Professionalization of Cataloging." *Technicalities* 13(5): 6–8.

Morris, Dilys E. 1992. "Staff Time and Costs for Cataloging." *Library Resources & Technical Services* 36: 79–95.

Rush, James E. 1994. "A Case for Eliminating Cataloging in the Individual Library." In *The Future Is Now: The Changing Face* of *Technical Services*. Dublin, Ohio: OCLC Online Computer Library Center, Inc., pp. 1–13.

Southeastern Library Network (SOLINET). 1995. *Workshop Schedule, Winter 1995*. Atlanta: SOLINET.

Thompson, Christine E. 1994. "NACO, OCLC, and the Catalog Department." *Rotunda: Newsletter for the University of Alabama Library Community* 8(16): 1.

Veaner, Allen B. 1994. "Paradigm Lost, Paradigm Regained? A Persistent Personnel Issue in Academic Librarianship, II." *College & Research Libraries* 55(5): 389–402.

9

Project Management and Organizational Change from the Advent to the Aftermath of Automation: Library and Cataloging Department Perspectives

Elaine Sanchez

INTRODUCTION

The initial installation of an integrated library system to automate library functions and services is becoming a distant memory for many libraries. Today, some are into their second or even third automated system. Most have gone beyond automation of basic functions to creating a system of information access that was not even a possibility when their libraries first ventured into library automation. The experiences and skills that libraries gain in the beginning of the automation project should help to build the basic project management approach and personnel and technical infrastructure to move into the later stages of automation. Library staff at the Albert B. Alkek Library of Southwest Texas State University have found that the things we learned, and the project structures we built, have enabled us to progress past the simple automation of library services and functions toward the integration of information access and the synergistic formation of new services, new technical capabilities, and new organizational structures.

As a result of automation, each functional area of the library had changes to make in its daily tasks, training environment, and organizational structure. The cataloging department at the Alkek Library was the first entire department to be directly involved in the automation process. As both creators and caretakers of the bibliographic, authority, and holdings databases upon which our integrated library system is based, we had a central role in the automation process. From the initial concept to our present stage of automation we have been a major player from the advent to the aftermath of automation. The projects we have been involved with have changed us forever, and for the better. I will describe the initial automation effort and some of the succeeding cataloging department projects we performed to demonstrate the management principles learned and applied. These management principles and the organizational changes that resulted from automation represent my own library's experience, but they can be used as models for similar organizational structures and for planning other library automation projects. Before going on to specific project management examples, a general explanation is needed to clarify what a project is, how it is managed, how project groups work and are led, and the role that information technology has played in leading libraries toward this type of management.

PROJECT MANAGEMENT, TEAMWORK, AND INFORMATION TECHNOLOGY

Each library's automation project is different from another's as each library has its own history, resources, personnel, goals, and organizational structure. These unique attributes cause each library to need different types and levels of decision-making groups, project staff, and automation project implementation plans. Even though the individual projects are different, several common management considerations exist that make library automation project planning and implementation more effective and successful. One first has to understand that the initial library automation project is a project, not an overall, ongoing working environment. There are several characteristics of a project, all of which apply to library automation projects:

1. Projects are temporary events with set objectives that are accomplished by organized use of the correct resources.

2. Projects require the simultaneous achievement of the performance specifications, the time schedule in which to complete the project, and the cost-budget estimate.

3. Each project is unique because it is done only once, is temporary, and usually involves a different group of people.

4. Projects are accomplished by resources—people and things—and many necessary resources are only minimally under the authority of the project manager. (Rosenau 1992: 1–5)

The above characteristics of a project, which also outline the role of project management, form a general definition that can assist planners of library automation projects to see the overall parameters of the work to be done. Just as projects are unique, though, so will each library's project management style and project definition be unique. The project manager and staff must take the lead and set out the management methods and project goals that can best work with local resources and that are acceptable to the administration.

The person who is chosen to lead this temporary grouping of people to achieve the undertaking of the library automation project has a large number of obstacles to overcome to successfully pull his (or her) team together to achieve the project. A project manager's tasks are these, according to Rosenau (1992: 8–11, 188–190):

1. Achieve project objectives in the organization despite pressures—often selling ideas to those in upper management;

2. Define the project's goals;

3. Plan how the manager and the team will meet performance requirements on time and with the chosen resources;

4. Lead all others involved with the project by positive motivation rather than by authority, by stimulating creativity and loyalty to the project and to team members, and by stressing communication, shared information, feedback and respect for each other and each other's ideas;

5. Monitor and measure progress toward goals, as well as to correct the path of work if it strays from set goals; and

6. Complete the project so that it meets all of the project goals.

Of course a library automation project may be seen as a number of smaller projects that must be accomplished in order to achieve the larger project goal of a fully integrated online library system. As there are a number of subprojects, so there must be a number of subproject managers, each dedicated to the functional project that he or she is attempting to complete. Since the library's online system is initially an automation of cataloging, circulation, acquisitions, and other library functional areas, it seems reasonable to assume that project leaders for these areas should be well acquainted with the history, staff, and work processes for their area of the project. In the Alkek Library's automation project, this was the case. Staff were all experienced and most had been employed in the library for several years. This experience allowed a thorough understanding of the library's needs. Within the departmental project teams, and the intra-departmental teams that accomplished larger objectives, there was an emphasis on teamwork, rather than a hierarachical and authoritarian distribution of authority. Project leaders, often but not always department heads, were knowledgeable in their areas, and delegated authority for decision making to team members on implementation teams. They encouraged participation and creativity in decision making and carried out feedback regarding project successes and failures in a timely manner for implementation success.

As it was exciting to be part of the change that automation brought within our own departments, it became even more exciting and important that each project manager and project team also understood the project goals of all other functional areas in order to achieve the larger goal of an integrated library system. Peggy Johnson states:

Information technology increases the comprehensibility of the very processes that have been automated. Any activity must first be broken down into its component parts and analyzed before being converted into computer transactions. This step prepares the way for automation as it simultaneously creates a deeper understanding of the activity itself. The technology that makes automation of library operations possible also creates an overview of organizational functioning. . . . Library managers can consciously exploit the new information presence to create a different and . . . insightful grasp of the library and its mission. This new understanding . . . can serve as the catalyst for . . . improvements and innovation in operations and services. (1991: 134–135)

Johnson's description of automation presenting an opportunity for improved organizational patterns can, indeed, be made to happen. Formal lines of work between acquisitions and cataloging have become less rigid as we both initiate our work on the same bibliographic record, which acquisitions initially transfers into our database, and we share the process of adding holdings for different types of materials. Circulation and cataloging must work together to withdraw materials attached to a patron's record, or to fix individual record values to reflect changing circulation needs. The interactions and responsibilities that our previously separate functional areas now share and work together on are proof to us that our integrated online system, and the information technology that started it, have drawn us irrevocably together for the provision of more complete and up-to-date information to our users.

INITIAL LIBRARY AUTOMATION PROJECT

We began systematic research into automated systems in 1987. This was, at first, only an upper management task. The Learning Resource Center director and the University Librarian, along with all department heads (acquisitions, administrative services, cataloging, circulation, and reference), performed the vital first steps in project planning. Starting the project with the full support and participation of high-level administrators ensured that our automation project would have the best chance for success, as "the most effective implementation projects have the full support of top-level administrators within the organization" (Johnson 1991: 106). We, the administrators, were the ones who initiated the Alkek Library's first steps toward automation project planning. We knew many of the advantages that an online library system offered, having seen a few online library systems and having read extensively about library automation projects. We also knew that state money was available for such projects and wanted to use that opportunity to benefit the library and the university.

Our initial project planning was in reality a feasibility study, even though we didn't identify it as such at the time. A feasibility study has several important purposes, which include:

1. Establish that a need for an automated system exists;
2. Define the goals of the automated system, based on the library's objectives;
3. Determine the costs, staff, and accuracy and quality of information of the system in use, whether manual or automated;
4. Describe or design a new system to achieve the objectives; and
5. Establish hardware and software requirements and request proposals. (Johnson 1991: 107–111).

The Alkek Library's library automation feasibility study consisted of the following actions. We:

1. Generally reviewed and analyzed other current library automation projects by way of site visits, working with an automation consultant from the Texas State Library, attending regional workshops on library automation, and reading other libraries' RFPs to identify reasons for our project, gather possible automation goals, and to validate our initial project plan;
2. Defined project proposals and identified automation goals that we wanted to achieve;
3. Reviewed the proposals and goals to determine their validity and consistency with our library goals;
4. Discussed the value of the project and its effect on library staff, workflow, and organization;
5. Identified primary limiting requirements that would affect the project proposal or its success, such as
   a. our limitation to a system operating with current campus computing services DEC equipment and a VMS operating system (hardware and software limitations);
   b. budgetary limitations (acquiring state funding for library automation projects);
   c. performance requirements, such as response time, system capacity, maintenance support and training, and operation of specified functions;
6. Identified primary strengths that would aid the proposal or its success, such as
   a. strong staff interest and abilities;
   b. availability of money for state-funded library automation projects;
   c. interest and support from the university computing services department;
   d. abundance of information on current library automation projects;
   e. other academic libraries within our Texas State University system were moving toward automation.

Once the initial project was validated and outlined, we began to look at possible options. There were several. We could enhance the current locally created circulation system, request a new local programming initiative to create an integrated system, or research library automation software vendors that could meet our needs and requirements. The three issues that enabled us to make an intelligent choice among the options formed what I later learned was called "the triple constraint" (Rosenau 1992: 15–22). We wanted a system that (1) would meet our performance specifications; (2) would be completed in a timely manner according to an agreed upon schedule; and (3) would fall within our cost constraints.

The same group of upper administrators made site visits to other libraries to see the operation of several systems. As we moved closer to a decision based on the constraint principle of performance requirements, we had an on-site demonstration for library staff of the system that most closely fit our performance specifications. Prior to this demonstration, library staff had seen other on-site library automation vendor demonstrations. However, staff were aware that this demo was the culmination of an initial automation project proposal that might lead to a future contract for a turnkey automation software package. We had, by use of general personnel management wisdom, taken the second action that helps to assure the success of a project. Throughout the project all library personnel were kept informed of its progress and the initial feasibility study results, and they were involved in the selection decision by soliciting their input after the demonstration.

As it turned out, library staff were pleased with the demonstration and with the library automation software package presented by the vendor. With staff backing, and the initial project plan indicating this vendor was able to meet our requirements, upper administration met and approved a decision to create an RFP. The RFP would state in great detail the definition of our library automation project in terms of the triple constraints of performance requirements, time schedule, and budget. This was the advent of our library automation project, and our first step into the organizational change that comes with automation.

CATALOGING DEPARTMENT AND THE LIBRARY AUTOMATION PROJECT

Cataloging staff were heavily involved in the following areas of the library automation project once the vendor was selected and we began to work on those actions needed to complete our online system. They included:

1. Technical aspects of specifications, selection, creation, loading, and integration of the bibliographic, authority, and item databases;
2. Structure of the indexing systems and record values for the same databases;
3. Integration of preexisting manual and automated cataloging, authority, and holdings data into the new databases;
4. Revision of cataloging and library material processing workflows;
5. Barcode specifications and barcoding projects, including barcode cleanup projects;

6. Training of library staff in the searching and use of online records in the new system; and

7. Integration of preexisting acquisitions, circulation, and reference functions and/or data into the online system when these functions dealt with records maintained by the cataloging department.

Each of these seven areas required multiple projects for completion and most were planned and directed by cataloging staff. The first major project was database creation, a project that really consisted of several tasks. These tasks were contingent upon each other, had certain time restraints built-in by vendor contracts, and mainly involved cataloging staff. The second major project, and the largest as all library staff were involved, was the barcoding project and the resulting barcode cleanup projects. I will describe the processes and general management of these two major projects, because they were examples of complex processes that incorporated effective project planning and implementation methods.

Database Creation Projects

The Alkek Library purchased DRA's ATLAS system in 1989, and began to prepare to bring up the system. Since I had personal responsibility for the cataloging department's portion of the project, I had staff begin reviewing system documentation and learning about the system even before it was available. We read the documentation and answered quiz questions that I had created to test our comprehension of each chapter. We met weekly to discuss the documentation, review our quiz questions, and ask questions, which I then asked of our DRA contact person. This advance preparation helped us lose some of our fears regarding the system, even though we could not as yet perceive how we would change our workflow to best utilize the new system.

Our first real step into the automation project began as we looked at the implementation schedule discussed with us by our DRA installation specialist. Database preparation and conversion was one of the first steps toward implementation of the system. I chose a small team of staff that had knowledge of the long history of cataloging practice at the library, computer programming and logic experience, and experience with authority control and physical processing. We called ourselves the Policy File Group, and we had several project goals that we had to achieve and coordinate with the appropriate library departments and with library upper administration. Our goals were:

1. to create the conversion tables that would translate text in certain fields of our MARC bibliographic records to item record locations and circulation values;

2. to decide upon indexing structures and defaults;

3. to ascertain those fields we wanted to match multiple versions of MARC records with, and how we wanted to de-dupe (remove duplicates from) our records;

4. to choose a method for correcting improperly tagged initial articles (so that titles would be sorted properly);

5. to set up circulation values for our to-be-created item records so that each volume and copy would have the correct format and shelf location in the online system, as well as the correct circulation limits;

6. to work with other library departments to help them convert their manual systems of shelf location (such as reserve), unique material formats (textbooks and curriculum guides, for example), and circulation data into the new item records;

7. to identify and select our smart barcode specifications; and

8. to establish spine and book label parameters for the online program that automated these physical processing activities.

We met weekly, and established activities that would give us the information we needed to complete our tasks, focusing on one goal at a time. As we finished a goal, we proceeded to the next until we had completed the overall project. The library administration coordinated our work with other departments. We discussed our recommendations with the library administration, as well as re-ported our progress and ideas to the DRA installation specialist during our proj-ect. Although it was new to us and was sometimes frustrating because we didn't always know if we were exactly right, we worked together, shared assignments and information, documented and verified our final results, and met deadlines set by our group to achieve our work.

With our first project achieved, the Policy File Project, we felt a strong sense of unity, pride, and team camaraderie. We also knew that we understood the system better, and that we were being truly creative in our exploration of un-known automation territory. Our next project was to determine what parameters we required for the authority records, which we had previously recommended for purchase and inclusion in our online system. The Policy File Group and I felt that this project should include more cataloging staff, as we wanted to get others in the department to start participating in the creation of our database. Extra people were added, both because they were needed to help with the work and to ensure that they would learn the new system.

With that belief, the Authority Database Group was created, and the Policy File Group disbanded until next needed. This authority group was larger and included myself, all six catalogers, four library assistant level IV's, and any library assistant level IIs who wished to attend. We had a DRA-supplied dead-line to meet so that we could request authority records according to their im-plementation timelines. Our project goal was to complete the authority record processing parameters that Blackwell North America (BNA) needed to create a tape of our authority records. The Authority Database Group reviewed the work-forms provided by BNA, and consulted with BNA staff to answer questions and determine standard options. In the process we again learned more about the system, learned to find the best choices for our library's online authority control, and began to claim our "ownership" of the authority database. Although some staff time in regular cataloging activities was lost because of activity in this group, it was worth it as part of the overall plan to include cataloging staff directly in the creation of their database.

Our MARC bibliographic records were extracted from OCLC, the bibliographic utility that held our electronic archival copies of the MARC records we had chosen for use in cataloging our collection. These MARC records were extracted and placed on on magnetic tape in 1989 and sent to DRA for bibliographic and item database creation according to our Policy File Group parameters. Copies of the bibliographic records tape were also sent to BNA for authority record processing and creation, according to our Authority Database Group parameters. Another copy was sent to our smart barcode vendor, Watson Labels, again with parameters decided on by the Policy File Group and the library administration. As we received each completed magnetic tape that would comprise our online system of bibliographic, authority, and item records, the university computing services department loaded them, and formed our new online system in late 1989. We were not able to catalog into or circulate using our new system, however, until July 14, 1990, which resulted in a long gap of OCLC cataloging not reflected in our online catalog. As a result we had to request a catch-up tape of bibliographic records for this gap from OCLC, send DRA our bibliographic and item record parameters, and initiate action to receive authority records from BNA and a second set of smart barcodes from Watson. We formed a short-term project group called Marion/Tempor Merge (Marion is the name of our bibliographic datafile and Tempor was the datafile of records cataloged during the gap) to determine the consequences of bringing in new and duplicate records. By now most cataloging staff had been involved in many aspects of the automation process, and I felt we could have a smaller group look at the issues. Catalogers and library assistant level IVs formed to meet and discuss the problems. We worked directly with our DRA installation specialist to answer questions, and arrived at a course of action based on our research and knowledge of our cataloging activities during the gap in cataloging. The Policy File Group reformed to go through the same decision-making processes for database creation as before.

After this final effort required for database creation and integrity of record information, we received our full complement of tapes, records, and smart barcodes by December 1991. Our databases were complete, our various database creation project groups had achieved their goals, and our cataloging staff was totally enthusiastic and involved in their usage of the online system.

Barcoding Projects

The barcoding projects were planned based on the use of smart barcodes that had author, title, call number, location code, and volume or copy data from the MARC record. Item records that corresponded to these smart barcodes were already in the online system. All we had to do was to place these corresponding smart barcodes on the matching physical pieces in the collection, and record for later resolution those titles with problems and those with multiple volumes or copies that had no corresponding smart barcodes. Since the scope of the project was large, more staff had to be involved in order to complete it in a timely fashion. Parameters were discussed with the university librarian and Smart Barcode Project team members were chosen from the entire library staff. Qualifications for the team included:

1. creativity and flexibility;
2. knowledge of selected area;
3. knowledge of circulation and shelving arrangements;
4. knowledge of divergent cataloging practices that would reveal themselves in smart barcode and related item record problems; and
5. willingness to participate.

Barcode-planning meetings were held weekly to keep momentum going and to keep our project on track. There were three key information distribution and control processes that allowed us to maintain focus and direction, as well as to document project goals, milestones, and decisions. These elements were the weekly agenda, the weekly action list, and the weekly meeting minutes. They were used during the entire planning process to ensure that we knew exactly where we were, what we had done, and why we did it that way.

The agenda for each weekly meeting set up milestones and goals for the various stages of our project. It kept us from straying too far from these goals and helped us maintain our planning schedule. Agenda topics were distributed before meetings to allow for individual research and thought that, in turn, enabled a more informed and a quicker decision-making process.

The action list was a weekly compilation of required project tasks that were assigned to members of the Smart Barcode Project. It was also an indicator of progress toward project goals. As we completed items on the action list, they were marked as achieved, and we all saw visually our project move forward step by step.

Minutes of the decisions and discussion of the prior week's meeting were reviewed for accuracy at each following meeting. This allowed us to review our decisions briefly and reconsider any that might not be as sound as first thought. Having a quick review was very important to the quality of our effort and we used it effectively as a quality-control technique. Project planning should include time for review and revision of planning decisions as projects are by nature risky ventures that often have no clear precedents to follow.

With our information distribution and control processes in place, our first action was to seek information on our current barcode placement practices and on other libraries' barcoding projects. This research made it possible to identify project parameters, determine necessary resources, and avoid problems that others had encountered. It gave us concrete examples of how others had barcoded their collections and made us clearly aware of what our current barcode placement practices were. In our case this analysis enabled us to improve and standardize our barcode placement guidelines so that we would ensure quality barcoding project results. After discussing the research results, we were able to create our project plan. The milestones to achieve were identified as:

1. project timeframe and milestones for project completion;
2. determine which library staff to include and how to organize and supervise for best results;
3. determine which statistics to keep, how to record them, and how to distribute to staff to show progress;
4. project problem resolution steps;
5. identify materials needed for completion of project, such as forms, folders for barcodes, and pencils;
6. design forms needed for the project to record problems for later clean-up, statistical counts of work completed, and work in progress—so staff know where to begin their barcoding shift;
7. divide stacks into manageable project areas, and coordinate with smart barcodes;
8. assign project staff responsibilities in the actual project;
9. determine procedures and documentation for barcode placement on materials, team barcoding method, and training sessions for library staff;
10. experiment with project materials and procedures to ensure that they would work; and
11. determine physical setup and location for barcode materials for library and project staff and barcode cleanup materials.

We completed our first barcoding project in about four months during the library's regular operating hours, employing several workstudy students and all library staff. We were able to do this as we were not yet circulating or cataloging on our new online system during this period.

Immediately after the first Smart Barcode Project, we began our first Smart Barcode Cleanup Project, using the problem forms that staff had completed in the first project. These forms noted barcodes that did not exactly match pieces, pieces that had no barcodes, and incorrectly placed barcodes. Support from the administration was sought and achieved as the Smart Barcode Project had been very successful; the collection was barcoded quickly and well, and our planning efforts kept everyone informed and involved. Because of this support we were able to involve all library staff again in this new project. The project goals were to correct existing item records that had been identified as problems, create item records and apply dumb barcodes to materials that did not have smart barcodes, and resolve any other problems remaining from the initial barcode project.

As we had done in the prior barcoding project, we employed our three information distribution and control processes of the weekly agenda, the action list, and the record of decisions and discussion for review and quality control. At our weekly planning meetings, we set our objectives, created the structure of the barcode cleanup effort, determined project staff involvement, wrote documentation and hand-outs for training, experimented with a small section of materials to ensure our plans would work, determined what statistics to keep, determined methods for keeping staff aware of progress, and then began our project. This particular project is still continuing in the area of complicated barcode problems and serial holdings, but all multivolume and multicopy monographic materials that were noted as problems in the first barcoding project were corrected.

There remained the Second Smart Barcode Project that occurred when we received the catch-up tape records. After that came the Second Smart Barcode Cleanup Project. The project management principles and the established infrastructure of project teams from our first barcoding projects had proven themselves successful, and we continued to employ them to sail us through these concluding barcode projects more easily.

CONCLUSION

The Albert B. Alkek Library staff, especially within the cataloging department, have had their large share of automation projects that began with the automation of our services and functions. We have learned much about project management and the related changes in organizational functions and structure that information technology brings. Staff participation and creativity, empowerment of staff in decision-making areas once reserved for higher management only, and an extension of the knowledge of library operations to all staff levels are but a few of the more exciting and promising changes. Our library's automation project allowed us to delve into other library-operating areas, learn their tasks, and analyze our own department's interaction with and integration into their once separate functions. I believe that Peggy Johnson's interpretation of the current environment and its meaning for the organizational future of libraries is right on target:

The increasing comprehension of library operations and the integration of those operations with new ways of thinking and making decisions about work have a structural impact on the library organization. Broad access to information and the immediate need to make decisions at all levels are redefining the system of authority in libraries and narrowing the gulf between library managers and the people they have supervised. More responsibility is being given to the individual to respond, and to respond creatively. (1991: 138)

The project management principles that I have identified in this chapter form a management environment that encourages and rewards creativity, flexibility, and more horizontal decision making in the automated library. They can also be used by other libraries to save themselves much preparatory time whether they are heading toward their first or their tenth automated system. The basic principles can be summarized as follows:

1. Get the active support of upper administration as these are the people that should set the organizational policy in support of automation, and as they are the main source for project resources;

2. Conduct a feasibility study that will establish the need for the project; define its goals; determine costs; analyze existing systems, including personnel and the manual or automated systems in place; design a new system, and establish hardware and software requirements as well as system performance specifications; and prepare for the creation of an RFP to begin the search for the system vendor of choice, if applicable;

3. Do extensive research, including site visits and gathering actual examples of other successful projects, to support the feasibility study and to serve as sources of information for your own local projects; consider hiring a consultant or seeking expert advice from your state library's automation division if one exists;

4. Recognize the temporary and unique nature of the project and the special leadership skills of positive motivation, rather than hierarchical authority, that the project leader needs in order to focus project staff and form a team that works well together;

5. Choose project team members that have the knowledge, experience, and qualities that will allow them to work well together;

6. Design and follow through on monitoring and measuring project progress, correcting deviations as soon as they are noticed;

7. Encourage the creation of interdepartmental teams to facilitate the integration of library services and to create new services and more flexible organizational structures;

8. Keep library staff informed and involved in the project as much as possible, seeking input at every opportunity;

9. Use the agenda, action list, and minutes of planning meeting decisions and discussion to form the information distribution and control processes for project planning meetings; and

10. Experiment with the planned project before actually going ahead with it to make sure it will work and to find problems before the project begins.

These ten basic principles were used in the Alkek Library's automation project, as well as the cataloging department's database creation and barcoding projects. The experiences of our automation project, and the project management principles that we learned, helped us through the difficult first automation effort. They continue to give us a practical and flexible structure to improve our existing operations and investigate future enhancements. These management principles can serve as guidelines for any library searching for structure in their automation process. They can also establish a more flexible and creative organizational structure, and, most importantly, create an environment that encourages innovation and the provision of quality service.

REFERENCES

Johnson, Peggy. 1991. *Automation and Organizational Change in Libraries.* Boston: G.K. Hall & Co.

Rosenau, Milton D., Jr. 1992. *Successful Project Management: A Step by Step Approach with Practical Examples.* New York: Van Nostrand Reinhold.

10

Issues in Managing Automated Cataloging

Myrtle Joseph and Nancy C. Fricke

Librarians have always sought technological aids to facilitate and enhance services to the user. For technical services (acquiring materials, organizing them, and providing bibliographic access), automation was and is the major development in the last 40 years. Automation allows items to be processed and ready for the user quickly and efficiently. The emergence of unit-record equipment in the 1930s, offline batch processing on computers in the 1960s, and online computerization in the 1970s represent a few of the more pronounced technological events in the course of library automation. With the advent of full online automation, job responsibilities and organizational structures in technical services began changing even more rapidly than in the past. Because the bulk of technical services work is production oriented, procedures derived from industrial production experience can now be introduced into the library.

In an automated environment library managers are paying close attention to production goals. At the same time, the bibliographic records in online databases should reflect accurately the library's holdings. As networking opens every library's Online Public Access Catalog (OPAC) to users anywhere, it is also important to pay careful attention to cataloging so that the local database reflects generally accepted rules and procedures and is consistent with other catalogs found through networking.

Since 1902, libraries have been able to order catalog cards from the Library of Congress (LC) Card Distribution Service. In addition to supplying cataloging copy in card format this service provided a built-in authority structure for names and subject headings. Although the cards saved time and effort in deriving cataloging information, only main entry cards were supplied, so subject headings, added entries, and call numbers had to be typed on each card. In 1968, the Machine Readable Cataloging (MARC) format was developed for automated systems. The Library of Congress developed the MARC format correctly believing that a common record structure and format would facilitate the exchange of bibliographic information electronically between libraries, groups of libraries, and systems, thus it made the cataloging process more cost-effective.

Studies have shown that staffing costs are from 85 percent to 90 percent of technical services budgets. An automated system can allow a smaller staff to process materials faster at a lower cost, a real boon to libraries in this age of cost cutting and staff reductions. The Library of Congress was correct, and budget reductions can be realized by using an automated system.

BIBLIOGRAPHIC UTILITIES

The term "bibliographic utility" identifies cooperatively based online systems or networks whose origins were in the sharing of cataloging data. At present, the three major bibliographic utilities in North America are Online Computer Library Center (OCLC), Western Library Network (WLN), and Research Libraries Information Network (RLIN). All use mainframes or clusters of minicomputers to support online cataloging by their participating libraries. OCLC was chartered in 1967 and went online in 1971.

Each database comprises millions of records, composed of the full extent, or at least a major portion of the LC MARC records, as well as other records in the MARC format contributed by participating libraries. For a fee, libraries can download needed records, sometimes directly to their local systems, thus reducing the amount of time professional staff have to spend in original cataloging.

Nowadays, the utilities have broadened their offerings to provide access to authority records, support for original cataloging, online editing capabilities, catalog card and shelf list production, subscriptions to magnetic tapes of any library's online cataloging, and electronic messaging for interlibrary loan.

SELECTING AN AUTOMATED SYSTEM

Whether a library is planning to purchase its first automated system or is planning a migration to a more advanced system, a study should be done to determine what operations will be automated and what the system should be able to do. Automated systems are either commercially developed turnkey integrated systems, or locally developed or single function stand-alone computers. Richard Boss believes a turnkey system is more cost-effective because the price includes all hardware, software, training, installation, and ongoing support (1990: 105).

Boss (1990), Cortez and Smorch (1993), Reynolds (1985), and Casey (1992) are good sources for assistance in selecting and purchasing an automated library system. The best way to judge a system is to visit a library where the preferred system is in operation.

RE-ENGINEERING AND WORKFLOW MANAGEMENT

The common thinking that computers can replace people doesn't work if libraries impose automation on the existing manual system. The flow of work and the movement of items through technical services will be affected by automation and the tasks that staff perform will change. The optimum way to redesign workflow in an automated system is to use the management concept of re-engineering—a complete restructuring of technical services operations. Hammer and Champy (1993: 32) define re-engineering as "the fundamental rethinking and radical redesign of business processes to achieve dramatic improvements in critical, contemporary measures of performance, such as cost, quality, service, and speed" (1993: 32). To re-engineer means that the library administration and staff need to be willing to look at what they do with a fresh eye rather than continuing "business as usual." Accomplishing a radical restructuring of workflow assumes employees have the creativity, vision, and training to take on new challenges. Another important element of re-engineering is that once a process is set up it must undergo continuous reevaluation and adjustment.

Every institution wants the best cataloging available at a reasonable price. There are ways to arrange a workflow that can result in actual money saved. At the same time, the obvious ways to save money may result in inconveniences or inefficiencies in the workflow—each institution needs to balance these needs against each other. (Fladland 1992: 40).

Hirshon claims that technical services will require a radical transformation to survive in an automated environment (1994: 15). Some automated libraries may decide they no longer need a separate cataloging department, and all operations that work with the bibliographic record become part of a continuous workflow. In that scenario, the previous cataloging unit becomes a bibliographic control unit charged with maintaining the online catalog.

Outsourcing

In some situations re-engineering could result in "outsourcing" and the elimination of in-house cataloging. Outsourcing is a term now appearing frequently in library literature, especially when cataloging costs and staff reductions are discussed. Outsourcing means that a library contracts out its cataloging and receives items ready for the shelves. It is not a new concept, and libraries have used LC-printed cards since the beginning of the century. For many years short-staffed school libraries and small public libraries have relied on catalog cards supplied by vendors or have received items already cataloged from a regional center. Most small, and many large, libraries should give outsourcing serious consideration because it can free professional time for the arduous and important work of maintaining the online catalog, and the higher challenges of the new online environment. Catalogers should be freed from performing routine tasks so their high-level organizational skills can be applied to making the online systems a success.

Outsourcing all of a library's cataloging is a radical step for academic libraries, however. Wright State University Library claims to be the first in the country to outsource all of its cataloging, including original and member copy. "Outsourcing also enabled us to increase substantially the quantity of material cataloged while simultaneously reducing costs" (Hirshon: 17).

A decision to outsource library cataloging will require careful planning, including a well-thought-out, precise cataloging profile (editing requirements) for the cataloging vendor. This is a good time to evaluate whether the amount of local editing can be reduced and still provide records that meet the access needs of the user. Outsourcing plans must also include attention to quality control and database maintenance.

Another form of re-engineering is having catalogers work from home using a modem to connect to the library's electronic system. Transferring books and other materials from library to home can be a major obstacle to this process but some libraries photocopy the title page and contents, and make notes for the at-home cataloger. This new management concept may not reduce costs since it requires purchase and maintenance of off-site equipment, but it does allow valuable professionals, whose life situation requires them to be at home, the possibility to continue working.

Re-engineering of the cataloging process assumes that no one model will work for all situations. When a library manager is ready to design a more efficient workflow the questions on the following pages should be considered.

What Is the Goal of Your Anticipated Redesign?

Current library literature emphasizes access to the bibliographic record and the physical item as the two most important goals for technical services. The chief reason for automating cataloging is to get records into an online catalog as quickly as possible by facilitating copyediting and physical processing of library materials. A second important goal is to cut processing costs. Properly managed automation can cut costs by eliminating redundant tasks and reducing professional staff costs. Staff reductions occur if vacant positions are not filled or staff are reassigned to public service areas. Some libraries will have other urgent reasons for adjusting workflow.

Who Will Design the Workflow?

Is workflow design the job of management and professional staff or should paraprofessionals also be part of the design process? For a successful outcome, all staff should participate and so attain a sense of ownership of the new procedures. Redesigning is not easy and requires careful planning. It is important that all involved understand the goals and are committed to make the reengineering work. With good planning, personnel should not feel threatened, but look on this as an exciting opportunity to make their work more rewarding.

Can the Cost of Utility Searches Be Reduced?

Optimum workflow design should eliminate repetitive searches of the bibliographic utility since it is costly to search more than once for the same item. For libraries that do in-house cataloging, as well as some original, two suggestions are:

• Search, then download records from the bibliographic utility directly into the local system to be edited; or,

• After the initial OCLC search, load records into OCLC's Cataloging Micro Enhancer (CAT ME Plus). Later these records can be updated and produced free of charge in non–prime time and added to the library's database.

Libraries that outsource cataloging will save money on utility searches because they may only have to search once, at the time of ordering.

When Will Your Library Do Copy Cataloging?

For libraries that do little or no outsourcing, editing of copy will be done when new items are added. Copy cataloging means using LC MARC records or another network library's cataloging copy, if available. When acceptable copy is found during acquisitions searching, library materials can be pre-cataloged before the items are received in the building. The cataloging copy can be edited to local specifications and a call number assigned. Authority work can be done and labels and shelf list cards can be generated and filed with the order forms.

If the precataloging records are released to the OPAC, the status would indicate "on order." In those libraries that are not outsourcing, materials received in the library can be barcoded and the ownership mark and security tapes applied immediately. Or, this physical processing step can be done after the item is checked against the OPAC record. If no further editing is required, the status is updated, the label is applied, and the item goes on to circulation.

A second search can be done after materials arrive in the library if a Cataloging in Publication (CIP) record was found during the acquisitions search.

Most of the time a full record will be available by the time materials are received.

Libraries using the Dewey Decimal Classification or libraries that do extensive editing of network-supplied records are more likely to want the item to be in hand for cataloging. Some records will not have a suggested Dewey number, or the suggested number will need to be adjusted to fit into a library's collection. Some Dewey libraries have special schemes for certain sections of the collection. In some ways, Dewey classification is more costly since it is nearly always done by librarians rather than paraprofessionals.

How Will Original Cataloging Be Handled?

Original cataloging means creating a record from scratch, a costly and time-consuming process. OCLC users find records for up to 95 percent of their acquisitions, and a similar rate is probable for other utilities. There will always be some items for which copy cannot be found or for which there are unacceptable records. Original cataloging must be supplied for these items and it is nearly always done by a professional librarian. Short-staffed libraries may put a provisional record in the OPAC and allow items to circulate, or they may prefer to store items like this for a period of time and do another search of the bibliographic utility in the hope that a record will have been added in the interim.

To best serve users, the first option is preferable. The value of materials diminishes the longer they are held from circulation; keyword searching in an OPAC will enable users to retrieve these items. Also, putting items on the circulating shelves is the cheapest storage and costly materials are not kept from users who need them. If the second option is chosen, a place must be found to store items waiting for original cataloging. If items are to be placed in storage, the library plan should state for how long a time they should be stored before doing another database search.

There are other sources to search for records not found in the utility. If the library owns national catalogs, such as National Union Catalog (NUC), British Museum Catalogue (BM), and Bibliothèque Nationale (BN), they can be searched for older books or foreign language books, or other online library catalogs can be accessed through the Internet.

Cataloging New Formats. As data obtained from electronic networks and other electronic information sources become more common, libraries will have to decide whether to catalog this information. Library managers will need to keep abreast of new cataloging rules for electronic information and other new formats.

Will Cataloging Be Done Directly on the Utility?

Copyediting can be done directly on the utility or a library can download records to be edited on the local system. Since it is expensive to provide a

terminal for each cataloger, sometimes librarians edit printouts of the bibliographic record and a staff person inputs necessary changes at a central terminal.
If local system terminals are less expensive to purchase and maintain than utility
terminals, a library might decide to have catalogers edit records on the local
system.

When Will a Bibliographic Record Be Added to Your Online Catalog?

If access is your primary goal, consider downloading records directly to the
OPAC as the materials are ordered. Status can indicate "on order" or "in
processing." The ability to add records to the online catalog at any time is
another benefit of automation. There will need to be a way for users to request
"on order" or "in processing" items, if the library decides to allow items to
circulate before they are fully processed.

Some libraries will still prefer to wait to release records to the OPAC until
the materials are completely processed and ready for the user. In this case,
materials should move quickly through the workflow and the cataloging backlog
should be minimal.

How Will You Separate Items as They Are Received?

If there is satisfactory copy available, or if precataloging has occurred, those
items can continue in a fast-track workflow. Decide what items are priority
cataloging—usually the newly received items or RUSH orders. Items needing
original cataloging, nonprint items, foreign language materials, and special collection materials are often processed separately. Staff with foreign language
skills and subject expertise may have such items assigned to them.

How Will Processing Tasks Be Assigned?

Making these decisions depends upon the number of staff available at different levels (students, clericals, technicians, paraprofessionals, professionals) and
the level of difficulty of the task. Sometimes lower-level staff are more receptive
to automation and quickly learn to manipulate records efficiently. Librarians can
devote time to bibliographic work and other professional activities, if they delegate routine cataloging tasks such as bibliographic utility searches, data entry,
and checking authority files to paraprofessionals. The trend is for librarians to
take on more of a training and supervisory role in the automated library.

How Will the Quality of the Local Database Be Maintained?

The Quality versus Quantity Debate. If access is the primary goal of technical
services, is it necessary to have a "perfect" bibliographic record for every item?

The quality versus quantity dilemma is difficult for librarians trained in traditional cataloging methods. But more and more, libraries are reducing the amount of editing of LC or member copy. However, library administrators will need to examine past practice and the extent of scholarly research the library supports, before making a decision to limit the amount of copyediting.

Each library needs to decide what local fields are essential. Can your library continue to do detailed editing of each record, such as deleting other libraries' call numbers, and still maintain production goals? It may be necessary to accept other catalogers work (member copy and LC copy), even if not perfect. It is really essential to update records from one set of cataloging rules to another? Consider whether some record, even if not perfect, is better than no record. If your decision is to edit each record to meet local standards, then you must also decide whether this is professional or paraprofessional work.

Authority Work. Authority control in cataloging means establishing uniform headings in a consistent structure for names, subjects, and series. Consistent headings are essential in a card environment, so that like items can be filed together in an alphabetical scheme; and they are important in an online environment as well. To achieve authority control, libraries have traditionally kept separate files for each kind of heading. With the advent of online systems, many libraries now have their authority files built into their systems to facilitate authority work.

Full authority work means checking every record against files for name, subject, and series. This is a labor-intensive, time-consuming operation, even when files are available on the system. Keeping three separate files up-to-date requires constant attention. Some libraries are cutting back in authority-control work because it seems less important with an online database and the availability of keyword searching. Some librarians have questioned the effort put into authority work and wonder if it really benefits the user. Smaller libraries, or any library suffering severe staff reductions, will want to consider dropping some, if not all, authority-control work. Series authority work especially seems less necessary in an automated library. Larger research libraries will likely continue authority work, but should consider maintaining files on the same system used for cataloging if not already doing so. Files can be either local and specific to the individual library, or they can be external and generalized. Some systems allow both.

If the decision is to continue authority work, consider the following points when planning how it will fit into the workflow:

- How much authority work is necessary for your library?

- When will authority work be done? Some large libraries have a separate authority-control unit, or an authority specialist, and checking is done pre- or post-cataloging. In an automated system catalogers can also check authority files as they catalog items.

- Who will do the work, librarians or staff? Library staff have been trained to search authority files in many libraries. If cataloging is outsourced, professionals have more time for authority work.

The Shelf List. The shelf list is another tradition now being questioned. Some automated libraries continue to order shelf list cards from the bibliographic utility, adding barcode(s) so that the shelf list can be used for inventorying the collection. Other libraries have decided that the shelf list can be managed on-line—especially if the automated system can provide call number browsing capability in order to display records in call number order. In this case a printout of records in call number order can be used for inventory purposes.

Other reasons for closing a shelf list are the need to control floor space that the shelf list files take up and the time it takes to maintain a manual file. If the decision is to close the shelf list, good database management is essential. A shelf list should not be closed until an inventory has been taken so that the library's database is an accurate record of library holdings.

Database Maintenance and Quality Checks. Libraries need to have a database maintenance unit or a librarian who is responsible for quality checks, correcting errors, and deleting records for items no longer in the collection. This unit may also revise records when additional copies or volumes are added. Some quality checks must be built into the workflow. There should be at least spot-checking of records going into the online catalog. Checking *every* record slows the release of records, and in some libraries delays patron access to new materials.

Copy cataloging done by paraprofessionals should be closely supervised and all work checked until the supervisor is satisfied with the quality of work. Often one librarian does the majority of checking so that common errors can be flagged. In some departments a casual over-the-shoulder occasional checking may be all that is needed. Or, professionals can check each others' work. When rule updates are published, or copy catalogers have questions, or a pattern of errors is occurring, consider holding a group problem-solving session to help in maintaining the cataloging quality. When a change in the classification scheme or new procedures are introduced, formal training and more careful checking may be necessary.

How Will the Cataloging Backlog Be Managed?

Sometimes libraries have a backlog of items awaiting processing before they can be released for circulation. The size of the backlog will depend upon factors such as:

• A large number of items received in a short period of time, usually due to a budget release that required large purchases in a limited time frame;
• A shortage of staff;

• Too much time spent editing cataloging copy; and

• An inefficient workflow.

One school of thought says there is nothing wrong with a manageable backlog, especially for times when there is a lull in the number of items being received. However, once a review appears people will want the item, a good reason to expedite material out of the backlog. In some academic disciplines, relevancy and currency have a limited time span of their own; so new material must be available before that time span is shortened significantly.

To keep a backlog under control, items should be moving continually into the cataloging workflow. If records were downloaded into the OPAC from time of ordering, they can be updated as materials leave the backlog area.

For libraries that store items needing original cataloging, they can be left for a short period—perhaps three to six months—while periodic searches are made in the database for a usable record. After an agreed upon time, they should be sent to catalogers for original cataloging if no record has been found.

Preparing a Workflow Chart

Many libraries produce a workflow chart that shows how materials flow through technical services from receiving to circulation, including stops to apply ownership marks, security tapes, barcodes, labels, and book covers. A flow chart can be useful in evaluating a library's workflow and when training staff for their particular tasks.

A workflow cannot remain static in this electronic era. There should be a continuous process of assessment and adjustment as new equipment updates and enhancements are added to library systems. Libraries should be prepared to make necessary changes in order to use expensive equipment to its full extent. Establishing a small task group to meet and review workflow periodically is one way to do continuous evaluation.

MANAGING LIBRARY STAFF TRAINING

Library managers must provide for adequate staff training in the new skills required to work in an automated environment. Training will be necessary in the following situations:

• Upon the installation of a new automated system or when system upgrades are installed;

• When new employees are hired or when library staff has been reassigned to cataloging from other library departments.

All staff need to know how their jobs fit into the overall workflow and the importance of doing their best to help meet cataloging goals. Persons new to cataloging will need training in bibliographic utility searching and the MARC record. They will also need to learn how to manipulate data in the editing process.

Training should take place as close as possible to the date when a new system is installed. Steps in the training process include identifying who needs specific training and who will provide the training. As paraprofessionals take on more of the cataloging process, librarians take on more of a training role.

When a new system is installed, those who are trained first can serve as trainers for others. Training manuals should be available from the vendor, but most libraries supplement the vendor materials with locally developed guides to introduce new equipment and new techniques. Contact other libraries using the same system to see if they have training materials you can use. To train cataloging staff:

- Provide practice on a test database with hands-on exercises at the computer terminal. This can reduce stress if fear of automation is rampant.
- Keep in mind how adults learn. A good training program should include a variety of training techniques. Working under close supervision, followed by a period of independent practice and experimentation, with a librarian near at hand to answer questions, is probably the most effective means of training; it is also the most costly.
- Be open to suggestions for additional training or for new ways to do a task.

Responsibility for training does not stop when everyone seems to have gained confidence in the use of the new system. Training must be scheduled when there is a new release or an upgrade is installed or a new procedure is being initiated. Staff can be kept informed of recent developments by circulating print memos, in-house newsletters, or e-mail.

The importance of structured training cannot be overemphasized. Some larger libraries have a training coordinator who is available to provide training on request. When staff are left to learn on a trial-and-error basis, they may not learn how to use the system to its full capacity. Furthermore, self-instructed staff may be teaching others incorrect procedures, or they may be unwilling to share what they know for fear they are doing it wrong.

CATALOGING WORK ENVIRONMENT

Managers must take steps to alleviate staff concerns about the work environment when automation is introduced. Computer technology in the library requires staff to spend more time in front of a computer screen—nearly the entire day in the cataloging unit. An unpleasant work environment and poorly designed individual workstations can affect productivity. Physical discomfort can lead to carelessness and errors. There are many sources to consult for information on ergonomics, or the relation between a worker and the work environment. Dyer and Morris (1990) and Dainoff and Dainoff (1986) discuss staff complaints about lighting, back and other physical pain, stress, and noise. They offer many suggestions to library managers on ways to alleviate staff discomfort.

Staff will have a sense of "ownership" if they participate in designing their workspace. It is good if they can visit well-designed offices in a nearby office building or on campus, or try out chairs and desks at an office furniture outlet. A scale drawing of the newly designed workspace should be displayed for several weeks, so that staff can check that workstations are in logical positions.

Managers must not become so involved in technology that they ignore the effect of stress concerns on previously good working relationships. Expect more conflicts among the staff and listen carefully as concerns are expressed. Good communication between management and staff is essential to avoid conflict and keep the workflow moving.

CONCLUSION

The advent of automation and the need to contain costs have changed library technical processing, leading to new management concerns. Another important factor to consider is that new information technologies have made users impatient for quick access to library materials. A cataloging process that does not have rapid access as its goal will not be serving its users adequately. Re-engineering techniques suggested in this chapter address access and cost control goals. To achieve both it may be necessary to give up or short-circuit some traditional cataloging processes, such as full-authority work.

Libraries must carefully plan the introduction and management of new technology. As we move into the twenty-first century, librarians and library managers must be prepared to take risks and try new ideas. Outsourcing all library cataloging is an innovation that shows great promise in helping libraries reach production goals while keeping costs in control.

REFERENCES

Boss, Richard W. 1990. *The Library Manager's Guide to Automation,* 3rd ed. Boston: G.K. Hall & Co.

Casey, M.H. 1992. "Getting the Best System for Your Library: Communication with Vendors." Proceedings of the Seventh Integrated Online Library Systems Meeting, New York.

Cortez, Edwin M., and Tom Smorch. 1993. *Planning Second Generation Automated Library Systems.* Westport, Conn.: Greenwood Press.

Dainoff, Marvin J., and Marilyn Hecht Dainoff. 1986. *People and Productivity: A Manager's Guide to Ergonomics in the Electronic Office.* Toronto: Holt, Rinehart and Winston (Canada).

Dyer, Hilary, and Anne Morris. 1990. *Human Aspects of Library Automation.* Brookfield, Vt.: Gower.

Fladland, Kathy. 1992. "Optimizing OCLC workflow in a Large Machine Computing Environment." *OCLC Micro* 8(4): 37–42.

Hammer, Michael, and James Champy. 1993. *Re-engineering the Corporation: A Manifesto for Business Revolution.* New York: HarperCollins.

Hirshon, Arnold. 1994. "The Lobster Quadrille: The Future of Technical Services in a Re-engineering World." In *The Future Is Now: The Changing Face of Technical Services.* Dublin, Ohio: OCLC Online Computer Library Center, Inc., pp. 14–20.

Reynolds, Dennis. 1985. *Library Automation Issues and Applications.* New York: Bowker.

SELECTED BIBLIOGRAPHY

Alley, Brian. 1988. "Reshaping Technical Services for Effective Staff Utilization." *Journal of Library Administration* 9(1): 105–110.

Association of Research Libraries. 1987. "Managing Copy Cataloging in ARL Libraries." In *SPEC Kit 136.* Washington D.C.: Office of Management Studies.

Association of Research Libraries. 1991. "Training of Technical Services Staff in the Automated Environment." In *SPEC Kit 171.* Washington D.C.: Office of Management Studies.

Bayne, Pauline S., Jillian Keally, and Joe C. Rader. 1994. "Implementing Computer-based Training for Library Staff." *Library Administration & Management* 8(2): 78–81.

Epple, Margie, Judy Gardner, and Robert T. Warwick. 1992. "Staff Training and Automated Systems: Twenty Tips for Success." *Journal of Academic Librarianship* 18(2): 87–89.

Estabrook, Leigh, Lisa Mason, and Sue Suelflow. 1992/93. "Managing the Work of Support Staff." *Library Trends* 41(2): 231–245.

Gorman, Michael. 1994. "Innocent Pleasures." In *The Future Is Now: The Changing Face of Technical Services.* Dublin, Ohio: OCLC Online Computer Library Center, Inc.

Hyslop, Colleen. 1994. "PrompCat Prototype: Accelerating Progress in Technical Services. In *The Future Is Now: The Changing Face of Technical Services.* Dublin, Ohio: OCLC Online Computer Library Center, Inc.

Intner, Sheila. 1994. "Outsourcing: What Does It Mean for Technical Services?" *Technicalities* 14(3): 3–5.

LeBlanc, James D. 1993. "Cataloging in the 1990s: Managing the Crisis (Mentality)." *Library Resources and Technical Services* 37(4): 423–433.

Picknally Camden, Beth, and Jean L. Cooper. 1994. "Controlling a Cataloging Backlog or Taming the Bibliographic Zoo." *Library Resources and Technical Services* 38(1): 64–71.

Rush, James E. 1994. "A Case for Eliminating Cataloging in the Individual Library." In *The Future Is Now: The Changing Face of Technical Services.* Dublin, Ohio: OCLC Online Computer Library Center, Inc.

Ten Have, Elizabeth, and Denise Forro. 1992. "Patron Access to On-order and In-process Titles." *College and Research Library News* 53 (11): 702–708.

11

Analysis and Maintenance of Database Integrity

Cassandra Brush

"Library automation" is a somewhat misleading phrase. The library itself, the building, the shelves, the various circulating and noncirculating materials are not what's being automated. Many library staff are currently involved with the automation of the various processes and tasks that comprise the functional structure of the system that is the library. We implement modules of systems that have offline antecedents. The Online Public Access Catalog (OPAC) has the card catalog as its antecedent, just as circulation, serials check-in, acquisitions, and technical services have their offline, paper-file antecedents. Transition from an offline to an online environment requires careful establishment of parameters. Parameters for consideration include the following three: lines of reporting as they exist prior to automation as well as changes that can be anticipated with the advent of automation; a rationale for the order of implementation of the various modules that make up the system; and consideration of procedures that will not be automated and whether they will remain within the department of their origin. Comprehension of the natural specialization that occurs within the library will facilitate useful change. Technology is changing so rapidly that it is often necessary to incorporate aspects of technologies not fully understood in order to implement them when they are needed. Software is designed to be user-friendly and transparent. The problem with transparency is that while the functionality may be transparent, the method and underlying structure is often opaque. This chapter will discuss the identification and resolution of errors in an OPAC. Topics of discussion will include union catalogs, offsite conversion,

Procedure	Archive Tape Updated	Local Files Updated
Cards modified	No	Yes
Online record updated, new cards ordered	Yes	Yes
Cards modified, online record updated	Yes	Yes

smart barcoding, and catataloging using the system. We'll begin where many began in the early to mid-1970s, with the union catalog.

THE NETWORKS

The Research Libraries Information Network (RLIN) and Online Computer Library Center (OCLC) are the two major union catalogs used for shared cataloging. RLIN is distinguished by retaining the display of an individual institution's revisions to existing records. The display of each institution's revised records reduces errors in the production of an archival tape of holdings because the contributing library can review input, make changes, and view results. This is not the case in OCLC, where there is a unit record that is modified temporarily on the screen; it is modified permanently only on the archival tape for that library. Review of a record that has been modified will reveal only the original record, as if it had never been modified.

This "invisible" updating is often the source of errors in a newly loaded database. The best librarians are bright, resourceful people accustomed to maximizing the efficiency of the tools at hand. The only local OCLC product for many libraries for many years was the computer-produced cards filed in the shelf list and the card catalog. Input errors were visible only on the cards. In the event of an error on the card, three scenarios could take place to correct it.

Either (1) the cards were modified, (2) the online resource was updated and new cards ordered from the modified record, or (3) the cards were modified locally and the online record was revised to reflect the correction. Only the last two scenarios result in a corrected archival tape. Pragmatic use of the system to produce locally relevant products did not require updating the database records that would end up on the archival tape. There was a charge for cards and sometimes long records with many tracings could generate sixteen or more cards for a title. Some catalogers didn't understand the importance of updating records because they didn't understand that these records would end up on an archival tape that would, at a later date, be critically important to the library. Such catalogers were using the bibliographic utility as a resource solely for catalog records and cards. This lack of proper updating filled the archival tape with serious errors.

The antecedents for the OCLC-produced cards were either the card sets received from the Library of Congress (LC), or locally typed card sets. The LC cards came in packs containing the number of cards necessary to generate separate cards for each of the tracings, but none of the headings were printed at the top of the cards. Before LC cards were available, libraries typed or wrote the entire card set. That process was not discontinued when LC cards began to be received because LC cards were not received for all materials.

The computer-produced cards printed with local modifications to the online bibliographic record in OCLC were an additional labor-saving element of the use of shared cataloging through a network. Catalogers no longer needed to type added entries and subjects across the top of main entry cards to provide those access points in the card catalog. Full card sets generated from the online record constituted a major improvement. The hidden part of this system, was the archival tape. Each "produce" command (the command to produce cards in OCLC), entered to generate a card set, also sent an update of the record to the institution's archival tape.

Old procedures for changing headings, call numbers, etc. were incorrectly applied to the computer-produced cards. A whited-out entry or a whited-out and typed over call number on a computer-produced card generally signals a local change not made to the archival tape and hence, not made to the local database generated from the archival tape. Unless there was an understanding of the importance of the archival tape, the OCLC database may not have been updated. This scenario gives us a useful tool for identifying a potential problem area: the computer-produced cards themselves. Prior to offsite conversion of the library's holdings on the shelf list cards to machine-readable form, the shelf list is reviewed to estimate the number of records to be converted as well as to note documentation practices that must be explained to the conversion vendor. At the point of viewing the shelf list, computer-produced cards that have whited-out entries can either be flagged (for review when the database is loaded), or they can be corrected on the archival tape by going online and updating each record before the tape is generated. Errors in matching smart barcodes generated from the library database tape to the books or in locating items from the local online catalog will often lead back to these manually revised shelf list cards. If material has been removed from one collection to another, in-house access points—the book label and the card set—may have been the only changes made to record the new locations. The archival tape will retain the old location and generate smart barcodes as well as local system items showing the previous location.

The ability to machine-produce catalog and shelf list cards made the typewriter obsolete for creation or modification of cards. Librarians and staff were able to exploit this "remote typewriter" metaphor further with the creation and production of authority cards for series, personal names, etc. However, authority records on OCLC could not be used to produce cards; the "produce" command only worked with a bibliographic record. Some librarians thought they found a way around this limitation by modifying a legitimate record to create an authority record; but in so doing, they added a "ghost" record to the archival tape. They ended up replacing the main entry in the bibliographic record with the heading for the authority record. Then, in order to produce this set of cards, a call number was entered; so a 099 (the three-digit numbers refer to MARC fields) for "series" replaced the 090 or 092 in the call number field, unless the series was "classed together." The Title field was used to record the series decision. If a series entry was made, then a Note field was added to indicate whether the series was classified together or separately. The remaining fields in the record were deleted and a card was produced for the authority file. Since the "produce" command in OCLC also updates the archival tape for every card produced, the bibliographic record used in order to produce the "new" card was overlaid with the authority card information on the archival tape. An example of the kind of exchange that takes place follows:

Bibliographic record
Call number: HN690.G66B4
Author: Beals, Alan R.
Title: Gopalpur, a South Indian Village / by Alan R. Beals
Publisher: New York: Holt, Rinehart and Winston, © 1962.
Collation: x, 100 p. : ill. ; 24 cm.
Series: Case studies in cultural anthropology
Note: Bibliography: p. 98–99.
Subject: Villages z India x Case studies.
Subject: Gopher, India

Series authority card record
Call number: Series
Title: Case studies in cultural anthropology.
Note: Made.
Note: Classes separately.

By the time the proper cards arrive at the library, an important step would have been eliminated in the cataloging and authority-control process, but the "ghost" record has become part of the archival tape record. The resultant local database bristles with these and other "time-savers."

Another "creative" use of OCLC was to use a record to which the library has attached holdings to create another record for an entirely different item, perhaps one of solely local interest, not appropriate for input into OCLC. Use of a record to which holdings have already been attached eliminated the first-time use (FTV) charge on OCLC. Unfortunately, it also overlaid information in that record. These inventive and creative practices enhanced access to portions of the collection, but they also created a mess to be dealt with later. The librarians, perennially short of staff and dealing with increased information needs from an ever-growing user population, dealt with this situation handily and practically. They had no idea of the problems they were creating as they solved the problems before them. The invisible archival tape, meanwhile, had bibliographic records overlaid by cross-references, authority records, or locally relevant materials for which cards had been generated. Early assessment of this phenomenon, coupled with procedures for replacement of the bibliographic record onto the archival tape, can reduce the number of errors found when the local database is created.

This assessment is obtained through in-depth interviews with staff on local procedures, documentation of those procedures, and discussion of former practices and procedures. For example, the library will have a current "profile" with OCLC. Part of that profile will be the holding codes for the various locations in the library. There may be earlier versions of the profile that contain holding codes that are no longer valid. Holding codes may have been established for previous locations that include brackets to clarify the code on the cards. It is important to know all of the permutations a given location has had in order for the local online catalog to accurately reflect all holdings now in that location.

Paul Crumlish's sidebar in a 1993 issue of *Library Hi Tech,* while focusing on the cleanup, mentions obsolete holding location codes: Former separate locations, such as Harvey Room and Jarvis Collection, may have merged with another to form the Janus Room. The location codes for all three coexist in the 049 field of the records. It is necessary to determine what has happened historically in the library since the advent of the shared national catalog. Only then can accurate specifications be given to the tape-conversion vendor who must be instructed to use the last holding location in the event that any of the three is found.

Crumlish also mentions typos as a problem in local notation that have the hapless library patron in search of the "RFE" instead of the "REF" collection (1993: 38–41).

Brian Sealy proposes documentation as a method for maintaining data integrity (1992: 25–34). His point that documentation should incorporate local policy matches my experience in the discovery of an unwritten policy while I assisted in the creation of local documentation of processes and procedures. Sealy's concern is for a consistent policy, through thorough documentation, in the local system. Inconsistencies in input prior to loading the local database lead to inconsistencies in that database. A lack of a common policy for a given situation, such as selecting a field for claims notes, will result in a confusing display for the library patron. For example, if claims notes are sometimes placed in acquisitions records and sometimes in volume holdings records, the resulting database will be difficult for staff and patrons to interpret. In an article, Brush details the varying forms that documentation can take (1991b). Valuable sources of information for resolving inconsistencies in the database include: a journal, procedural documentation, a timeline, and meeting minutes.

One of the services provided by OCLC consortia is to update regional serials holdings lists for resource sharing. Local data records in the Union List of Serials in OCLC are created for the member libraries from shelflist cards or periodical holding lists. One of the problems with this updating solution is that the individual libraries often will not have incorporated regular updates of the union list into their procedures. The creation of a local data record in the union list automatically adds holdings to the bibliographic record and writes the record to the archival tape. For this one-time update of the union list to be worthwhile, it must be maintained consistently. The library staff must incorporate updating the union lists into their procedures and documentation for serials records maintenance; otherwise, following updating of the regional list, withdrawal of a title may not result in deleting holdings for that title because no procedure was created. "Ghost" records may be the result of offsite updating from lists or shelflist cards.

It is important, if possible, to enlist the aid of the same staff who developed the card production techniques that generated unforeseen errors in the cleanup of those errors. The same enthusiasm and maximization of resources that motivated these librarians can be harnessed to address the problems that were created, and they will have a greater understanding of what is involved. This time, "problem solution" should not also result in "problem creation." Those staff will be aware of the various areas in the collection that need to be targeted for review once the problem is understood.

In the initial stages of evaluation and system selection, something as simple as the reordering of procedures may prevent further problems in the database while preserving the same efficiency as producing the cards in a batch which the others once did.

Authority files can be reviewed for computer-produced cards since it is known that these cards were produced from bibliographic records and are not true authority records. Later cards display the OCLC number of the bibliographic record enabling the library staff to retrieve that record from the national database.

The procedure developed at one site for this review and correction was as follows:

1. Search bibliographic records on OCLC from the OCLC record number printed on the bottom of the computer-produced cards in the authority file.

2. Print each bibliographic record found.

3. Check the LC call numbers on the cards in the local shelflist. (While the library occasionally varies from the LC call number in the online record, most problems will be located this way.)

4. Search the card catalog under both main entry and title for any cards that lacked an LC call number, or where no corresponding shelflist card was found in step 3.

5. Once the library-assigned call number is obtained, retrieve the shelflist cards with the bibliographic record.

6. Search OCLC for the bibliographic records matching the shelflist cards.

7. Make necessary changes to the online unit record from the shelflist card to update the record.

This procedure will update the archival records prior to the production of an archival tape for creation of the local database. Were the discovery not made until after the database load, an additional step would be needed to then overlay the local record with the modified OCLC record.

The same creativity that went into the development of the timesaving devices will work equally well at analysis and project development once the underlying problems are understood. The aspects of change theory discussed in Peggy Johnson's book *Automation and Organizational Change in Libraries* should be understood here (1991). It is especially important at the beginning, when staff knowledge of the system is low, to make them aware of their areas of expertise and the continuing validity of that expertise. Of course, it is also important to point out new kinds of information that must be learned. If technical services librarians had all understood the importance of the integrity of the computer database as well as the integrity of the card catalog, many costly errors could have been avoided.

OFF-SITE CONVERSION

The archival tape will consist of the last fifteen to twenty years of painstaking online cataloging and probably (depending upon the age of the library and the collection) half again as many titles converted offsite using shelflist cards. At one site, the OCLC holdings consisted of 35,000 records prior to off-site conversion. After the conversion, which had been done using OCLC and the shelflist from the site, OCLC holdings totalled over 100,000 records.

Some of those shelflist cards may have hastily composed "dashed on" entries with information such as: —c.2, Hodder and Stoughton, or —c.3 1945. The fact that the "copy" has variant publication information (in this case, the date) indicates there should be a separate record since the item is a new edition, and not merely a copy. The conversion team can be instructed to regard these *annotated* copies as variant editions, and search records for them. Unfortunately, all variant-edition "copies" might not be annotated with the distinguishing information. Offsite conversion staff, working only from the cards, have no choice but to add them as multiple copies in the appropriate field when multiple, undistinguished copies are indicated on the shelflist.

The initial evaluation period prior to off-site conversion should entail a thorough examination of the shelflist to see that the materials indeed match the cards. Quality-control projects may be developed to check multicopy titles for variant editions.

There are two ways to handle this, dependent upon available staff. In either case, the "copies" that are really editions requiring a separate record can be identified. Shelflist cards indicating multiple-copy holdings can be compared to the books to ensure the validity of the notation. When the notation is invalid, i.e., the work is a separate edition, the distinguishing element (publisher, date, etc.) should be noted on the original card for the conversion staff. When the notation is valid, that should be marked on the card so the local staff will add holdings to the appropriate record. The more errors that are identified before conversion begins, the less cleanup there will be after conversion is completed and when the barcodes are applied to the books. Otherwise, many of these errors will result in major problems.

Since off-site conversion is generally done prior to local database creation, records may not be viewed until after the local database is loaded. Libraries often send portions of their shelflist at a time so that all classification does not have to cease for the life of the project. If off-site conversion is being done on OCLC online via Microenhancer software, there will be conversion-edited records in machine-readable form for viewing purposes. Once these records are loaded to OCLC, the edits are still invisible online, but the Microenhancer software for editing and batch uploading the records retains the edited record file, and that can be printed or sent to the library on diskette.

We asked to see fifty records from every six drawers of the shelflist as the drawers were completed and returned to the library. This was a useful method of tracking the conversion to be certain that specifications were being met. Review of these records turned up very few call number problems. Library staff were able to make some corrections by updating the records on OCLC before the archival tape was cut. This was done as the printouts were compared to the returned shelflist records. Our request for the edited records that were to be uploaded to OCLC gave us a management tool to ensure the integrity of the shelflist.

Errors that cropped up during the smart barcode application included transposition of numbers in the call number (BJ1192.W65 input as BJ1912.W65) and miskeying classification letters. There was a run of several cards in one part of the BV classification where BJ was substituted for BV in the call numbers. These smart barcodes, of course, matched no books on the shelf. When these were compared to the card catalog, the error was quickly revealed and the correct call number entered in the local record; then the barcodes applied to the right books. Errors having to do with call numbers are high priority because they block access to the materials. Prioritization of error correction will naturally follow the seriousness of the type of error. An error in the abbreviation of a publisher's name is seldom important. Errors in the call numbers, authors, titles, or other access points will prevent retrieval of those records and are thus important.

Local conversion "cleanup" at the collection site follows off-site conversion. Correcting a record for a title is facilitated by the availability of the actual material described in the record. A shelflist card lacking publisher or date information may have been flagged by the off-site conversion team because multiple records existed in the national database that matched the card. Staff working on conversion cleanup can select the correct record by matching it to the physical item in the library. This cleanup brings "retrospective conversion" into the local arena and technical services must allocate resources to complete the conversion. On-site retrospective conversion presents its own paradigm of problems as described in Jay Lambrecht's excellent 1990 article. Lambrecht discussed the various stages, strategies, and tools for the analysis of such conversion projects.

The choices for database cleanup are to employ a vendor for off-site retrospective conversion or to attempt to do it locally based, in part, on the number of staff available. Typically, technical services staff numbers are proportionate to the number of annual acquisitions. Adding to technical services staff for in-house conversion involves training that will take resources from current cataloging work. Adding the conversion work to the existing workload of technical services staff will reduce staff for cataloging. The question becomes, "Is it more important to catalog older materials than to keep up with new materials?"

The age of the collection, the needs of the user population of the collection, and the relative value of the older and newer materials to those needs also are factors for consideration. If the current acquisitions are already accumulating into a dreaded "backlog," technical services staff won't be able to manage both a conversion project and current cataloging. If staff can be increased by one or two people working solely on conversion, a conversion project can be accomplished slowly. Larger conversion teams can be hired temporarily to complete the first stages more quickly, but the library must have space and OCLC or RLIN terminals available for the team. With the advent of client-server technology in the library, many library networks are able to provide national database access to standard desktop workstations, which simplifies this problem. And, the last consideration is the cost of hiring extra staff versus the cost for off-site retrospective conversion.

SMART BARCODES

Many of the database problems will become evident as the smart barcodes, if they are used, are matched to the items the records represent. Smart barcodes are generated from the call number, local holdings, and author and title fields of individual records in the database. Call number, author, or title information on the smart barcodes, when it fails to match the actual works, signals the need for database error correction.

The tape vendor typically scans the 049 field of the MARC record for holdings. Volumes and copies are recorded there and marked by the appropriate subfield delimiters. The vendor will create a separate field for each component item of a title, while the vendor of the local online system will create the item records associated with the title. However, many libraries didn't initially use the 049 field to record copies and volumes. Typically, the tape-conversion vendor will scan the 300 field (containing the collation, in the MARC record) as well, in order to cover the possibility that there is no information in the 049 field. If there is no information in the 049 field, and the pagination subfield of the 300 field indicates pages only, then only one field will be created to represent that title. If there is no information in the 049 field and the 300 field does contain volume information, then the number of volumes will be taken from there, and separate fields will be created for each of the volumes found. The problem with this approach is that any missing volumes from a multivolume set will have smart barcodes generated; these barcodes will then appear to be errors. It is important not to discard these extra barcodes because they represent actual records in the database. Smart barcodes can become a tool for quickly retrieving and deleting items that have no physical volumes present. Error-report forms should indicate clearly where extra barcodes are needed and when too many have been generated, as well as any discrepant call number, author, or title. After the bulk of the collection has been barcoded, these forms become useful tools for error correction.

The road to automation is not the place to start discarding all paper files. Now, more than ever, every file is a check and the more paper files available, the saner librarians will remain while trying to solve problems. The library may even want to lengthen the normal retention period for some files; files reflecting the months during transition can be boxed and stored. Worksheets from months during which transitions in procedures occurred are particularly vital and should be kept in chronological order and clearly labeled. They might almost be cataloged.

CATALOGING USING THE SYSTEM

In the course of using the newly loaded database, errors in authority control and access points will be discovered. The particular parameters of the local automation system may dictate a specific formatting for call number or location information. The shelflist will be, next to the materials themselves, the library's primary control over the online database. Until the collection is fully converted, the shelflist will be necessary for assigning call numbers, which is no doubt one of the reasons the paper shelflist is one of the last files to be automated.

Materials that use an accession number for the call number rather than Dewey or LC classification may be made accessible by material type, if that code is added to the call number. Tape-conversion vendors can be instructed to move bracketed media-type codes, translate holding codes, and insert this information with the accession number—but invariably records with neither of these distinguishing factors exist. A call number search in the local system will retrieve an alphanumeric sort of all call numbers in the database that begin with numbers. So the search "find call   " or "c =   " will show numeric call numbers first. This isn't much help in a Dewey-classified collection; but in an LC-classified collection, the numeric 099 fields will display first and if the appropriate material type has been added, it can be searched. The addition of the material type in front of the number also allows users to browse, via call numbers, videos, cassettes, compact discs, and other materials.

Another call number problem results from overgeneralization of the recommendation to retain all data. In the local-catalog MARC record, it is important to delete *indexed fields* that contain irrelevant information. Many libraries using LC classification retain the LC classification number in the 050, or Library of Congress–assigned, call number field, if that classification number "fits" in the local shelflist. In the event that the cutter number has to be altered (a date added or other local changes need to be made to resolve conflicts with local shelflisting), an 090 field that represents the *local Library of Congress classification number* is created. Both fields are indexed in the local database to allow for retention or modification of an existing LC call number. If the 050 field is not deleted when the 090 field is present, both call numbers will be accessed during a call number search. Only the 090 will contain a call number for an actual book. To avoid this, it will be important to specify to conversion vendors and local catalogers to delete the 050 field if a local call number field is generated. Some lessons are learned the hard way; I actually requested the retention of the 050 fields in the records at one site to monitor local versus LC practice. Naturally, once the database was loaded and the multiple-access problem was revealed, this practice was stopped and future edits to any record included scanning the record for the presence of both fields.

This type of problem is well suited to machine processing. Processing code may assume the following logic: IF record number = X, where X = the range of record numbers in the database contains field 050, AND IF record number X contains field 090, THEN delete tag, indicators, and date for field 050. The X can be set to increment to the next record number and the job set to run at a convenient time. Online catalogs allow this kind of processing. Any project that involves inspection of more than 1,000 records for a single change is better done by computer than by hand.

Libraries often will have a second copy of a reference title in the circulating collection. The method for specifying holdings for a title that is in more than one location in the MARC format is to list the second, third, and later holding codes in separate subfields "a" of the 049 field. Because the initial subfield "a" does not display and is not input in an OCLC record, the concept of stringing that particular subfield was often misunderstood. Consequently, records were updated with the holding code for the additional location(s) in place of the main location code. The resulting item representation at the local level will be only for the last updating. A correct 049 field for a title in the main collection and the reference collection should be formatted: 049 CUST$aCUSA, where CUST is the holding code for the main collection and CUSA is the holding code for the reference collection. An updated record with the formatting 049 CUSA, will cause an item to be created for the reference collection but none created for the main collection. Then, during barcoding, a "dumb" barcode with no call number, author, or title information will need to be applied to the volume in the circulating collection and this will need to be wanded (with a barcode reader) into the system so that the holdings will be correctly represented in the local catalog.

It is preferable to become aware of and master as many problem areas as possible for implementing the circulation module. Methods for dealing with specific problems can then be given to the disk workers, speeding their mastery of those problems. Most systems will accommodate "on the fly" circulation of unconverted materials; brief title and call number information can be entered for an item and it can be barcoded for circulation. When the item is returned, it will be routed to cataloging by virtue of its "on the fly" status. Cataloging staff can determine by consulting the shelflist if a new record is needed for the title or if one already exists. If smart barcoding had been done, a book lacking a barcode will indicate that the record for the book is part of the conversion cleanup or that there is a smart barcode error. Technical services staff can then check the online catalog and offline files to determine what the problem is and to correct it.

Simple browsing of the indexes will turn up typographical errors as will searching on lists of commonly misspelled words (Ballard and Lifshin 1992: 139–145).

SUMMARY

Careful documentation of procedures prior to automation or migration will facilitate an objective analysis of effectiveness. It may also reveal flaws that may create access problems in the database. Both long- and short-term effects of current local practices need to be understood fully by the people who will be documenting and performing them.

Offsite conversion projects should be carefully monitored to assure data integrity. A preliminary review of the method used for conversion will reduce errors. Regular communication with the vendor will familiarize the vendor's staff with everything you know about your database and minimize errors they might make.

The library staff is the most valuable part of the organization and the frontline to access. Confidence that they can improve their value and usefulness is an important part of the transition to a new automation system.

While not "self-correcting," most library automation systems will assist in the discovery of problems. Increased access will bring long-buried problems from the depths of card catalogs or accession lists to the computer screen, while improved error-correction functions will facilitate resolution of those problems. The automation librarian needs to be aware that maintenance initially will demand more time.

The shelflist, printouts of conversion records, cataloging worksheets, smart barcodes, error reports from the smart barcoding, and the database itself are tools to build the best database that can be created.

It is important for the systems manager, public and technical managers, the staff, and the director to share a vision of the goals of the library and of the clear paths to those goals. In order to do this, it is critical for the involved parties to retreat from the mundane aspects of database maintenance, cataloging, circulation, report generation, serials check-in, and so on to review and direct patterns and overall direction of the automation process. Analysis and documentation can often fall by the wayside in short-staffed libraries, further increasing the problem of inadequate staffing by rendering the current staff less efficient. Looking at the "big picture," we see that review of the literature on implementation should trigger ideas and methodologies that will facilitate project design for database cleanup. Proper time allocation and prioritization will allow an effective system librarian to be involved in the daily aspects of system use while maintaining a grasp of the future implications of local policy decisions. The same methodology will allocate time for the managers to review literature and incorporate into their workflow planning techniques that occur with this analysis. With analysis and workflow design an integral part of the process, new products, such as smart barcodes, will be recognized and utilized as fully analytical tools in addition to their primary function.

Publius, writing in the first century B.C., reminds us, "It is a bad plan that admits of no modification." The commitment to frequent analysis will enable the automation librarian to change direction when that change is warranted. Changes in the order of system-module implementation, hierarchies with the library, reporting patterns, content of reports, and so on may be matched to the pattern of development. That pattern will be readily observed if planning and analysis are an integral and ongoing part of managing the library in general as well as managing library automation.

REFERENCES

Ballard, Terry, and Arthur Lifshin. 1992. "Prediction of OPAC Spelling Errors Through a Keyword Inventory." *Information Technology and Libraries* (June): 139–145.

Brush, Cassandra. 1991a. "Documenting the Implementation of an Integrated Online Library System." *Information Today* 8(7) (July): 8.

Brush, Cassandra. 1991b. "Methodology for Determining Database Integrity for Your Newly Loaded Database: Error Detection and Recognition." Proceedings of the Sixth Integrated Online Library Systems Meeting, pp. 11–18.

Crumlish, Paul W. 1993. "Garbage In No Longer Means Garbage Out." *Library Hi Tech* 44(11): 4, 38–41.

Johnson, Peggy. 1991. *Automation and Organizational Change in Libraries.* Boston: G.K. Hall & Co.

Lambrecht, Jay H. 1990. "Revising a Retrospective Conversion Project: Strategies to Complete the Task." *College & Research Libraries* (January): 27–32.

Sealy, Brian. 1992. "Maintaining Data Integrity by Documenting the System: Putting Databases in Writing." *Library Hi Tech* 39(10): 3, 25–34.

PART III

Keeping Up with Library Automation

Opening Part III, Howard Graves, systems librarian/cataloger, offers some words of advice from his experience. Time management, planning, and continuing education—self-improvement in matters of automation—are critical to successful performance.

In Chapter 13, volume co-editor Gerard B. McCabe discusses the best configuration of a library building to offer most usability of the new electronic information services. Experienced library consultants have identified the need for a new paradigm for academic library buildings. As libraries move into the electronic and teaching library concept, modifications of space will assist in providing the services smoothly and efficiently. McCabe notes the variety of options that academic libraries are using to accommodate full-service workstations from which students can access not only their library's online catalog, but local databases, catalogs, and databases of other libraries, by moving through the Internet and the World Wide Web as well. The modifications that some libraries will require are borne out by his brief report of a recent building experience.

In the concluding chapters, two former graduate students in Clarion's Department of Library Science offer overviews of recent literature. In Chapter 14, Catherine S. Cervarich presents bibliographic material covering system migration. The editors found it particularly striking that the literature on migration of online systems is growing; however, as noted in the introduction to this volume, many libraries have yet to go beyond participation in shared cataloging through OCLC. Her review of articles concerned with timing of a change is interesting to the editors too, because of the experience at Clarion where, as noted in the Introduction to this volume, replacement efforts for an eight-year-old system was just getting underway at the editing of these chapter manuscripts. In Chapter 15, Rhonda Ames looks at literature for managing integrated library systems. Good consistent management of integrated systems is essential. Ames's review is characterized by judicious selection of pertinent quotations from the literature's authors. Reading this chapter will provide readers with a concise summary of useful advice from people who are deeply involved in the daily management of complicated systems.

12

Time, Money, and Smarts: How to Survive without Enough

Howard Graves

An old Marine saying goes, "We've done so much with so little for so long, that I'm now convinced we can do anything with nothing at all." The first part of this adage sounds a little like library automation: too little time, too little money, too little expertise. Automating library operations effectively despite these limitations is the trick. Though we may not be able to duplicate the second part of the adage, some basic management principles, modified somewhat for the library automation environment, can be used to create systems that work.

Organization, delegation, time management, and setting priorities are management principles that are discussed throughout the three sections below. Good organization, to some extent, encompasses the other three principles mentioned above. Much is written about organization at the institutional level but it is every bit as important at the individual level. Well-organized institutions maximize their measurable outputs (product or service); well-organized individuals do the same, or in common parlance, they get more done.

Who hasn't heard the advice to delegate? Who's followed this advice? Everyone knows you can do it better or faster yourself. But should you? Constantly evaluate daily tasks with the expressed intent of delegating them. It is highly unlikely that you will delegate yourself out of a job. Instead, you will be constantly creating a new job with all the challenges and excitement that goes along with this type of change.

Have you ever watched what a good football team can accomplish in the last two minutes of a half or game? Coaches call this the two-minute drill and the success with which it is done separates the good from the excellent. It would be difficult and counter-productive to work each day at the frenetic pace of a football team's two-minute drill; however, by treating time as a resource to be carefully managed, you will be more productive.

Anyone with more to do than time permits must set priorities. It's part of the work life of anyone working in a modern organization. The effective manager uses knowledge of colleagues and the organization to set priorities intelligently, thereby maximizing effectiveness.

Discipline and persistence are individual traits that vitalize or energize theoretical management principles. They give these principles life. Consider them good habits instead of genetic inheritance, and work hard to develop them because they will prove their value every day.

What follows is the practical embodiment of these principles in daily work with library systems. Much of it is common sense, perhaps because these principles are distilled from the experience of successful people and organizations. They are as germane to library systems management as to management within a Fortune 500 company.

TOO LITTLE TIME

The most important rule in time management is: do it now. It is also the rule that is broken most often, usually because there is just too much to do and too little now. Setting priorities, working in an organized, efficient manner, and delegating tasks whenever possible will help maximize the now.

Setting priorities requires a solid knowledge of the library's goals and culture seasoned with a dash of reality. Because libraries are service organizations, user satisfaction must be the library's number-one priority. Equipment or systems used by the public, therefore, are automatically the number-one priority. Preparing for a system upgrade in your office is probably one of the most important responsibilities of a system manager when the big picture is being considered. However, if a key terminal, PC, or even a printer in a public area is malfunctioning, it will require immediate attention because at that moment the public cares more about their printed citation than a system upgrade that would meet their every need. Call it situational priorities, if you will. Preparation for that system upgrade, however, must not be neglected. The urgent (jammed printer) and the important (upgrade planning) must be balanced.

The priority of public demands over organizational demands is obvious. Less obvious, however, is setting priorities on competing back-office demands. Which comes first, the library director's question about replying to an Internet list, an OCLC network problem, loading the new software on the local area network (LAN), or the word-processing font problem? It depends. Is the director seeking information to resolve an urgent budget or personnel issue? Can OCLC be accessed at all? How long has the new LAN software been on the corner of your desk? Are the fonts to be used for an important library publication or a greeting card? All factors, such as the people involved, the time of day, and the urgency of the request, must be taken into consideration as priorities are set. All of these are judgment calls, so work hard to know your library and librarians so that good judgments can be made.

No discussion about priorities would be complete without a mention of squeaky wheels. You know the type—demanding, insistent, persistent, and perhaps even whiny. Their demands may not be more important than other demands on your time, but they cannot be convinced of this. Evaluate their requests in the context of the needs of the library user and other library staff. When they squeak on behalf of a user service that needs attention or a vital administrative function, grease away. When they squeak on behalf of a personal concern (because they are constitutionally unable to see needs other than their own), turn away. However, resign yourself to fact that the squeaky wheel in your library will get more grease because you are human with tolerance levels that change from day to day. Apply it as objectively as possible, trying not to neglect those with legitimate needs who ask only once. You may even suggest to the quiet that they find ways to keep you aware of their needs such as gentle reminders via e-mail or brief telephone calls, but not the dreaded squeak. Develop the discipline to go about your business cognizant of the needs of the organization and the individuals' needs as they further organizational goals despite the few who, quite frankly, pester.

Good organization will maximize the amount of things that can be done in a set period of time. Keep a list of tasks to be done and review it often. Hardcopy and electronic planners are available. At the most basic level, this list will prevent you from simply forgetting to do something, but this list should be more. It should include notations of actions taken on continuing projects, for example, the date of an e-mail message sent. It might also include key telephone and beeper numbers or the complete text of error messages. Keeping all this information in one place saves time that is often wasted looking in file drawers and through the jumble of papers that accumulate on desks. Reviewing the list will prompt a vital action: follow-up. Never assume a single telephone or e-mail message will precipitate the action you need. Your demands are probably competing with many others, so make sure they are receiving attention. When a task is complete, put a check mark next to it, or cross it out and revel in the satisfaction.

Sometimes, someone will call with a problem. Talk them through it on the telephone whenever possible and save on travel time. Know when to give up with the telephone. Don't try and talk someone through file transfer protocol (ftp) if they can't format a disk. Before you hang up and hit the road, however, make sure that the problem has been explained in detail. This puts some of the onus for the solution on the person with the problem. It will also help you prepare everything you need to get the job done, so that repeated trips back to your office for backup copies of software, blank disks, small screwdrivers, or your specially modified paper clip can be avoided.

Communicate answers to recurring questions widely and often. If you are frequently asked how to address an e-mail message to an Internet address, or how to post, subscribe, or set "no-mail" to a "listserv" newsgroup, anticipate that others have the same questions and answer them before they are asked. Electronic bulletin boards are great for this type of communication since they often permit some interaction that goes beyond sender and receiver. These forums may facilitate branching out beyond the basics to other useful commands or techniques. Continuing with the examples above, you may be able to branch out to the "mail reply" or the use of signature files. Searching "listserv" archives before posting or retrieving the registered participants of a "listserv," may prove useful to some in your library. The trick is getting people to consult these electronic forums. To encourage use, they must become part of daily routine, and this will only happen if useful information is regularly available and/or the conversation is lively. Reach those not so persuaded by using e-mail distribution lists. Any conversation that may develop here will be private, at least at the beginning, but your messages will demand a modicum of attention.

Delegating responsibility will maximize your time in the long run. In the short run, it will be a pain and probably not seem worth the effort. Several principles of delegation should be observed: give boundaries, ask for progress reports, give the necessary level of authority, and always follow up. Study your responsibilities closely to determine what can be delegated. That printer jam or the terminal that has been "adjusted" by a creative user are good starting points. Delegation can go further. At the start of any new task, nothing seems routine. Over time, however, patterns develop that can be broken down to component parts that are relatively simple. For example, designing a spreadsheet is your job; inputting numbers can be delegated. It is easy to fall in love with your spreadsheet and forget the second step. Once inputs have been determined, system reports and notices should be run in the department that uses them.

Delegating some computer-related responsibilities will pose unique challenges. First, you may feel uncomfortable delegating responsibilities that you have just mastered. Perhaps you have fought your way through a manual, tested a piece of software, and derived the desired output. You can get the job done, but you are not an expert. Delegating this responsibility may carry the risk that someone else will become more of an expert than you in this area and that can be threatening. Delegate it and expect to be in this situation with increasing frequency. Accept the fact that you may not know all of your organization's hardware and software as intimately as those who use it and have the temerity to tweak it. Second, some relatively simple and repetitive operations can only be done from a privileged account. Editing and submitting irregular batch jobs or simple editing of key files may require a privileged account. Basic security principles forbid sharing account information so it would seem this is a dead end. Depending on your tolerance for risk, however, it may be possible to bend this rule a bit by logging on to the privileged account and allowing someone you trust to use the account in a clearly specified way. Log it out promptly upon completion and your exposure is minimal.

TOO LITTLE MONEY

Spend wisely. To do so, prioritize, tap local experts, shop, as whenever possible, bargain.

Knowing the needs and capabilities of users and library staff is essential in establishing priorities. Just as with your time, library users and staff may be competing for the same limited resources. How does one choose between these competing needs? Should the users' needs always take precedence over the librarians' needs? Not always. One can make a case that money spent to equip librarians with, for instance, network access is leveraged to the ultimate benefit of users as librarians can practice and learn the nuances of applications that the public will also be using. However, spending to further automate the bureaucratic infrastructure must be avoided since this does not benefit users in any significant way.

Assuming that the proper balance between staff and users' needs has been established, how does one prioritize users' needs? As more data becomes available in electronic form, this will become increasingly difficult. Now almost all subject areas have electronic information offerings, often with print counterparts that may already be in the library. Know your public, scrutinize the data, and test the interface. Librarians have been buying based on their knowledge of users' needs forever. It is no different in an electronic environment. Librarians are also experienced in scrutinizing data in the hard-copy environment. Usually this is done by analyzing expert reviews, the reputation and credentials of the editor or author, and the reputation of the publisher. This is a good deal more difficult in the electronic environment since the reviewing mechanisms are not fully mature and there are many new publishers. When in doubt, it may be advisable to sample and analyze the information. Become the expert reviewer. Finally, a bad interface can doom good information. Make sure it is intuitive, powerful without being overwhelming to the new users, and capable of offering context-sensitive help that really helps.

Get help from local experts. Campus, municipal, or county computer experts should be consulted. Often they are making the same types of purchasing decisions as you, and they have already compiled and evaluated information and shopped around. There is little reason to believe that your decisions would be different unless your needs differ. Try to develop contacts with experts in the marketplace (salespeople, vendors). Once you have confidence that you are getting real information and not just a sales pitch, these contacts can prove useful; they may have access to new hardware developments and pricing information that could help you time your buying decision to the library's best advantage. For example, they may know that the latest-model laser printer with improved features at a comparable price to the old model is being released next month.

You would naturally wait and get more for your money as a result of this important contact.

The conventional wisdom in computer shopping is to buy the most powerful machine you can afford because you'll need the power tomorrow if not today. This is not always the case. Some people you buy for may never do anything more than process words or prepare simple spreadsheets. They could probably do this with a hand-me-down PC with a 286 processor; a 386 processor could surely handle these jobs; and a low-end 486 processor would handle these jobs and provide room for growth. If you know people's needs this well (and you should make it your business to), either "buy down" where the deals are, or "buy up" for your power-user(s) and utilize old machine(s) for tasks appropriate to their configuration. Supply people with the hardware that will permit them to do their jobs and do not anticipate growing hardware needs, unless there is clearly demonstrated capability. One exception to this rule is the LAN environment. Here, a 286 processor running local applications effectively may not behave as reliably when network-overhead places additional demands on PC memory and video components. Place your hand-me-downs carefully in such an environment.

The same principle should be used for some service functions. For example, buy down for services that are predominantly terminal emulation or for database searching, where the processing is done on a powerful server rather than on a workstation.

It is also time to accept the fact that computers have a definitive life that is not nearly as long as you would like. They may be at the end of their effective life after three or four years. Use after this time period should be considered a bonus. It is unlikely that we will see machines used as long as the OCLC Beehive terminals ever again.

There is room for negotiating with many of the database publishers as they struggle to establish pricing for their products. This is especially true for publishers that work in the traditional print and electronic environments. Sometimes the electronic product is based in large part on the data gathered for the print product so the revenue expected from the entire process is not predicated on the sale of the electronic product. This creates negotiating room. For much the same reason, there is also room to negotiate network licenses. A publisher could not expect a library to buy, for example, eight copies of a printed reference source, so why not permit some flexibility for an eight-user license for the electronic equivalent? The negotiating room for network licenses is the difference between the minimum and the maximum amount of extra revenue the publisher expects from a network license. Consider printed prices the way you consider an automobile's "sticker price." They are starting points, not ending points. Convince the publisher that you want to arrive at a fair price and that you will strictly respect the terms of the license by enforcing policy and/or by software-imposed limitations to the data.

Longer-term commitments to a product may also translate into savings. Some products are so vital to the needs of the library's users (these products will vary from library to library depending on the users) that two-, three-, or even four-year commitments can be made. Discounts should be available and negotiated in these situations.

TOO LITTLE EXPERTISE

Many active librarians in the field now went to library school when libraries contained just books. Some recent graduates emerge without enough technical expertise to choose hardware and run systems. They may be able to search OCLC, Dialog, or be familiar with the Silver Platter CD interface, but they may be unfamiliar with modem connections, telecommunications options, or MS-DOS extensions. That hardware decision or that system is your responsibility now, so you'd better find a way to get smart. Don't be intimidated by device drivers, NLMs, T1 lines, and routers, you can learn computing the same way you learned other subjects: networking, reading, and taking courses. Whatever method or combination of methods you choose, be persistent—that light will go on.

Networking in this context means people. Make as many contacts with people who know computing as possible, sort of like study buddies. They may be in your library or in some support unit of a larger organization to which your library belongs. Most are willing, some even eager, to share information. These contacts will become truly valuable if they develop into relationships, i.e., two-way interactions that entail trust and consideration of each other's time constraints. Like any relationship, these too require work and a willingness to give. Look for opportunities to give, perhaps you can supply information available in the library to someone outside. A favor here or there (a photocopy, a little research, and so on) can go a long way in building a relationship. Understand that your concern may not be a high priority and have patience, which is in such short supply in most organizations that it is always appreciated. Don't make every request an emergency and you will probably engender some trust so that a real emergency will be treated as such.

Use a huge network to network. There is more technical expertise available on the Internet than anywhere else, so get connected. One of the most active portions of the Internet are "listserv" groups, which are subject-oriented electronic discussions. Questions or comments are posted and responses from other list members usually follow. Monitor lists that deal with topics that are important to you. Learn how to search the list archives that might contain the answer to a question. Ask when you need information; supply information when you can.

Read everything about computing you can. There are books, journals, and online information available about all mainstream software and hardware. Networking and telecommunications are also receiving widespread attention in the printed media. Some of this writing might seem inaccessible at first. This might be because you don't possess the necessary technical background to understand the concepts; it might be because of bad writing. Stick with it. Read different authors on the same topic. Each time a small piece of the puzzle will be filled until it is complete and you are ready to move on. This takes time and persistence but it will happen, and with each success you go forward better prepared for the next puzzle.

Courses are offered in many places: your professional organization, libraries, library schools, adult education in school districts, and commercially. The American Library Association and its divisions offer courses in conjunction with annual and mid-winter meetings. Regional, state, and local library organizations are also active in continuing education. Try some of them. Some will be too advanced, some too basic; some will cover too little, some too much; some instructors will be better than others. Persist here too, as something can be gained from each of these learning opportunities. Go with questions and ask them, even if you must use a break and corner the instructor. Practice what you have learned as soon as possible after the course to reinforce the information. Review the course outline or other material distributed and try to reconstruct the main points covered. This probably sounds like work—and it is. Remember, you have some ground to make up on the computer types and this is one way to do it.

CONCLUSION

Can a traditionally trained librarian survive in a modern automated library? Without doubt. With some work and utilizing the organizational skills that are such a large part of our training, librarians can survive and excel. We can choose electronic information and run systems of excellence that meet the information needs of users. We can equip librarians and other library staff with computing and telecommunications equipment that help them meet the information needs of users. We can help prepare our libraries for the twenty-first century and beyond. It will take lots of hard work to master basics and lots more to keep up, but it can be done. As the ad reads, "Just do it."

SELECTED BIBLIOGRAPHY

Cochran, J. Wesley. 1991. *Time Management Handbook for Librarians.* Westport, Conn.: Greenwood Press.
Covey, Stephen R. 1994. "First Things First." *Success* 41: 8A–8D.
Kanarek, Lisa. 1993. "All in a Day's Planner." *Office Systems* 10: 34–38.
Levine, Gene. 1994. "Finding Time." *Bobbin* 35: 113–114.
Marquand, Barbara. 1993. "Effective Delegation." *Manage* 45: 10–12.
Peters, John. 1993. "On Time Management." *Management Decisions* 31: 66.
Ramsey, Robert D. 1994. "Work Smarter and Save Time." *Supervision* 55: 14–16.
Straub, Joseph T. 1993. "Managing Priorities and Deadlines." *Supervisory Management* 38: 3.

13

The Information Server Library: Toward a Paradigm for the Future

Gerard B. McCabe

The rapid continuing advance in the use by libraries of telecommunication and computer technology . . . will modify considerably internal library operation, and architectural and structural techniques will facilitate the advent of these modifications. (Kaser 1988: 160)

INTRODUCTION

The inspiration for this chapter comes from a paper by Murray Martin (1994) in which he addresses the need for serious thinking on the future library building. Although his concern is for the academic library, his rationale is applicable to all types of libraries. Regardless of type, library managers must plan for the newly recognized future, for high-level electronic information services. In his opening paragraph Martin quotes David Kaser, internationally recognized library building consultant. The sentence at the top of this chapter follows the sentence that Martin quoted. Both Kaser and Martin are emphasizing the need to find a new paradigm for the academic library building. Throughout his paper Martin remarks on the necessity of finding a new way of organizing library services, of reconsidering the way libraries appear today, and of rethinking how services are presented to users.

Planning the new or renovated library building for successful use of computer-based information services is the subject of this chapter. Unless we have effective functional surroundings we cannot succeed, so goes the timeless theme of library building planning. This chapter may offer a small step toward a new paradigm for library buildings: adapting them for the best provision of electronic information services. While information services rather than the building define the electronic library, the building needs to be designed to facilitate the provision of electronic information services.

THE CONCERN AND THE ISSUE

Our concern begins with conceptualization of the library building of the future in connection with electronic information services—whether you are planning a new building or scheduling one for renovation. The question, a serious management issue, of melding past and future needs must be faced now as the new Information Age gains momentum and improved technologies appear with increasing frequency. The services of the library expand on those of the 1960s, when automation was introduced for batch processing functions, and of the early 1970s, when online information services began. Now as we address more online computer-based information sources, a myriad of problems confront us. In his literature survey, Martin comments on the writings of Boss, Beckman, Kaser, Novak, Oringdulph, and a few other authoritative figures; he returns repeatedly to the need for change, for a new concept for the library building, and for one that must be a clear step toward addressing these issues of providing service in an era of high-speed information delivery, and for a clientele that expects nothing less than a stellar performance. The challenge is the same for all library managers; our library buildings or spaces must be functional, and they must facilitate the advancing services our clients are seeking.

In planning the new or renovated library building (or space), accommodations for electronic information technology should be designed so that users' efforts can be channeled directly and quickly to the end objective of gaining information. A chart diagraming how the typical user may approach access to library resources will assist this planning (see Figure 13.1). By physically arranging services in priority order, the library can provide for more of its users efficiently. In this new approach, all main floor services relate directly to users' needs. Nondirect services including administrative offices, technical services, and others—even the current periodicals collection, if its space needs interfere with those of reference and information services, may be located on other floors.

APPEARANCES

Traditionally, the library building opens with the circulation function immediately apparent, followed by the collection catalog and the reference and information services. This is so ingrained that often we can think of no other way to begin a library design planning effort, but the new library should open with information services side by side with the circulation-control function (with auxiliary functions relegated to other areas or spaces). We might visualize the library

Figure 13.1
Accessing Library Holdings Online/Offline

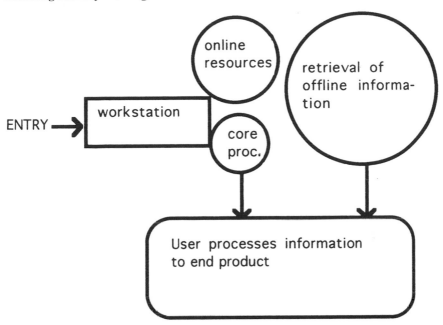

The user enters the library and begins work at a full-access workstation. The core processor channels communications to and from online resources. When this process is completed, the user gathers offline information elsewhere in the library and then goes to a location, a word-processing software–equipped workstation, to prepare the end product, perhaps a term paper or a technical report.

entry with public information workstations immediately past the lobby, and one or more staff strategically placed there to guide those users who need routine assistance. Librarians who will assist with complex matters are placed nearby at their own workstations. This is the central information service Martin refers to replace the now vanished card catalog area (1994) and it is the logical place to begin using the library (see Figure 13.2). To address this new need, some new or recently renovated libraries are grouping these workstations near reference and information services.

In some libraries, workstations within the reference and information services area are online database access stations and offer no software for processing information into some sort of workable format, e.g., a term paper. From these stations the online catalog, local online databases, and the Internet may be accessed. Students or users may download citations or other information onto a personal floppy disk. Elsewhere in the library building, there may be other full-access workstations, processing-only workstations, and offline workstations that contain word processing and other software.

Figure 13.2
The Library Services Arrangement

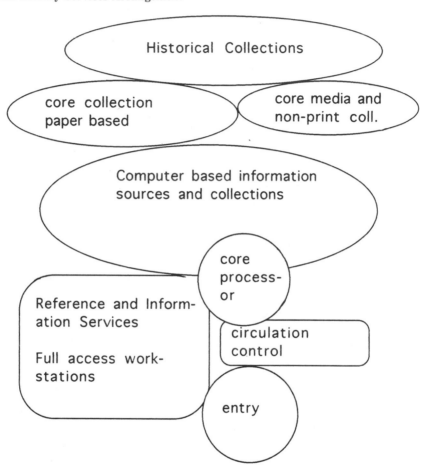

The user enters the library and proceeds directly to reference and information services, where he or she begins searching for information at a full-access workstation. The online catalog, other online local databases, and the Internet are all accessed at this station. The core processor handles all communications to and from online resources, and processes circulation transactions and technical services procedures. The user may download collected information to a floppy disk, and then either go to a laboratory workstation or to an independent workstation in order to begin processing the collected information. The library's other resources are located further into the library.

In another approach, some libraries have workstations assembled in a laboratory format. The variations may be: (1) all these stations are full access with supporting software for processing, or (2) all stations are equipped only with the processing software needed to refine collected information into term papers or reports complete with illustrations, graphs, tables, or charts. In this second instance, full-access workstations are located at the reference services and information and possibly in other library spaces.

The libraries also vary in their solutions to printing requirements. Very few have all microcomputers connected to a central printing room. In this case, printing options may be offered, dot-matrix or laser; for the latter, a fee may be imposed for cost recovery.

In other libraries, microcomputer workstations are complete with their own printers, either one-to-one or so many to a printer that is usually at the same work space or at one nearby. In some libraries, I saw little concern for noise. The printers were fairly quiet and no cabinet was used. Some expense, cost of cabinets or sound barriers, is saved and the paper was readily available.

Usually, disk drives are available right at the workstation, sometimes part of the microcomputer, or as an accessory. Another option for students completing assignments is to download the assignment for online transfer to a faculty workstation or to a disk that is carried to class and given to the instructor.

Local preferences for workstation orientation will vary among college and university libraries. The solutions just described all work. The decision depends upon or is influenced by the role of the library in its institution's teaching mission, the size of the library building, and traditional campus practices regarding methods of study or using the library. This chapter is not advocating any one solution to meet the need for electronic information delivery, but is stating that the need must be met.

The full-service public workstations provide access to the Online Public Access Catalog (OPAC), the library's online catalog. They also provide access to the library's serial and periodical databases, to local online databases, and finally, to the Information Highway—used here as a generic term encompassing the National Information Infrastructure, which gives access to the National Research and Education Network (NREN) and so to the Internet and the World Wide Web (see Figure 13.3). With this last access, users can search for information in off-site databases, including the catalogs of other libraries and information databases not housed on-site. A user or student may download information to a floppy disk for later recall. If all or part of the information obtained isn't available in-house or on-site, a user may call up, on the monitor screen, an interlibrary loan request form to initiate a request. After a few minutes, a user is ready to leave or move further into the library to seek and use its other resources.

Within the library, users may access stored holdings, use print materials at a reader station, and perhaps take notes on their personal electronic notebooks or laptop computers. For extensive copying of print materials, optical character

Figure 13.3
The Library and the Networks

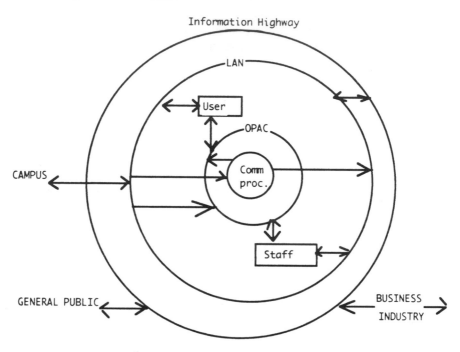

The Information Highway includes the Internet and NREN, and is part of the National
Information Infrastructure.

recognition (OCR) equipment provided by the library may be helpful to students.
The library should caution all users, however, about the copyright law. Although
a student research paper may not be intended for publication, students should
learn about reasonable and legal limits to quoting other works. The options
should allow for disk transfers or for printing either in the immediate location
or via online to a remote printer service, from which users obtain the finished
products and pay any fee involved. Similarly, users outside the library may
access through the communications system—local, regional, or wide area network—the same information, which lacks only the immediacy of the library's
holdings (see Figure 13.4).

POWER AND COMMUNICATIONS

Martin points out the need for greater electrification (1994: 94, 101); Beckman
remarks on the need for conduits and floor or ceiling grids (1990: 408).

The extent of power and communication connections should be decided very
early in the planning process. In planning for a new multistory building, this

Figure 13.4
The Central Information Service with the Library as Distributor

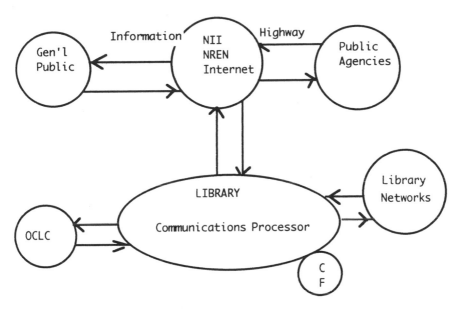

The library furnishes information to other public services, and to the general public through the National Information Infrastructure (NII). The NREN and the Internet are part of the infrastructure.

The library's relationship with OCLC continues as it presently exists; in some cases access to OCLC services may occur over the Internet, or if it is replaced then over the NREN.

The computer facility (CF) may be part of the library or it may be a separate entity that works with the library.

The library's relationship with other libraries in network arrangements continues.

decision must be made early so that if connections are to reach upper floors, they are planned for at initial construction and not added later at greater expense. Some conduits or ducts for possible future use may prove useful many years later. Time spent just thinking about meeting future requirements will pay dividends later in cost savings. Fiber-optic cabling, high-speed copper wiring, power lines, and telephone lines in floors and walls, depending upon workstation locations, should be required—as is the provision for ease of upgrading and working on the system. Means of supplying or accommodating these necessities can be found in such sources as manufacturers' catalogs or the Sweet's catalog.[1] The choice will depend upon need, cost, and construction specifications. For new construction, conduits or walker ducts can be placed in concrete floors; for renovation projects, options may be more limited, but raised floors and other solutions are possible. If ceiling heights permit, existing floors can be raised from less than three inches to as high as six inches, the choice depending upon the connectors required. Grading access to such a room can be accomplished with a gradual ramp that will meet the requirements of the Americans with Disabilities Act (1991). These conduits or ducts may be equipped with fiber-optic cabling, which connects microcomputers and terminals to category five, high-speed copper wiring. Sometimes rather than lay wire or cable in these conveyors, 200-pound test string is placed for use later in order to pull wire or cable through the conveyors. Staff requirements for connection to information sources also should be in the plan.

The new or renovated building requires a power supply sufficient to operate lighting, heating, ventilating and air conditioning units (HVAC), photocopiers, other machines, and the equipment that comprises or supports workstations. For the various small machines that are used in libraries, including items for personal use, Elaine Cohen recommends a rule-of-thumb of five amps per machine and cautions against underestimating the need (1994: 552–553). For estimating the proper capacity for the heating, ventilating, and cooling system one rule-of-thumb is to project the average human occupancy and then add one human equivalent for every heat-generating machine, including photocopiers, micro-computers, and printers. Using many circuits helps control competition for power. To provide adequately for information workstations and their peripheral equipments' power supply, safeguards against power outages are essential.

For the modern library and its power-dependent electronic information services, power independence would be ideal, but power losses or brownouts often are unavoidable, so precautions are required. Freedom from fear of losing computer files, of downtime, of inconvenienced users, and of wasted time would be wonderful.

When power outages occur, the need is for an uninterruptible power supply (UPS), which will allow a reasonable time for closing computer files and safely shutting down sensitive equipment. A fuel- or battery-operated generator may meet this requirement. In some geographical areas with plentiful sunshine, a backup solar power system may be feasible. New developments are occurring in solar-generated power that may prove worthwhile for supplying backup power for the information services. When commercial sources are under stress from severe weather conditions or production failures, an alternative source could help resolve some shortfalls in the power supply. In this new environment of seemingly constant online activity, there is no affordance for power outages and the serious consequences of lost work. The building project should provide for backup power sources; a minimal two-hour capacity is recommended. Electronic information systems are time-savers, but to allow even a first-year student to lose work toward a term paper through lack of an adequate backup system is unthinkable. For graduate students and faculty working on complex research projects, the loss of time can do incalculable damage. Sometimes power outages catch people unaware, and some advance precautionary measures are really crucial.

It is simple to visualize a computer communications processor of no great bulk that is sized for the needs of the library, through which all telecommunications activity passes and that routes the signals appropriately to the sources to be accessed. (Figures 13.1 and 13.2 show this conceptualization.) Depending upon the library's size and the actual needs of the community, the library may house its supporting computer center or have an auxiliary connection to a large computer center; either case provides the essential backup support for the operating services.

USER STATIONS

The flexibility of current library planning allows local preferences to influence user accommodations. Libraries can be found with microcomputer workstations of varying capabilities scattered through the building, while others have laboratories with cumulations of microcomputers. Whatever the choice, the user workstation usually will appear in more than one configuration. Some libraries are designing their own electronic workstations.[2]

Surface workspace can be a crucial issue. Student preference for individual or group work, or both, will dictate furniture choices. A mix of surface sizes may be best, but if 75 percent or more of observed student use of online services involves two or more students, then the wise choice will be the larger work surface, which will hold a microcomputer, printer, and library materials for all the students who may be involved.

STAFFING

Why are the workstations separated, with information workstations near the entry and processing workstations elsewhere? Why not simply have the same workstation do everything? The campus enrollment and the library's consequent size may be the deciding factor in workstation arrangements. The medium- to large-size library may find the laboratory arrangement preferable because technical assistance staff can be concentrated to help students. In a large building, it may not be efficient to have processing workstations scattered throughout seating areas. In a small library, either option may work, depending upon economies of space, staffing, and campus preferences. This technical assistance staff can consist of student assistants, possibly from computer-dependent disciplines, such as computer science, accounting, mathematics, or statistics.

THE MANAGERIAL DECISION PROCESS

Before deciding on the workstation configuration other than at the reference and information services, library managers need to evaluate campus needs carefully. Deciding the issue of having a central laboratory and how its workstations are configured requires understanding of several factors:

- Students' use preferences, whether independently, or in groups, which are encouraged by team assignments.

- Space availability and the availability of good environmental conditions, which means the HVAC system must be superior, especially if a laboratory solution is selected.

- Staffing with technically skilled workers. If academic programs produce a corps of potential student assistants to serve as technical staff for a laboratory situation, then student assistants from these programs can be used (Heck and Baker 1995). Depending upon the size of the laboratory, one or two permanent staff members will be needed to supervise.

- The separation of the full-access workstations for information gathering only from the processing software-equipped workstations.

The full-access information workstations at the reference and information services area are intended for the accumulation of information from specific sources. This approach provides for one or more librarians who are available to assist users in gathering as much information as possible from these sources. The librarians do not assist with word processing or other needs, though, leaving that to the technical staff; hence, at least one technical staff person and computer-knowledgeable student assistants are needed. After gathering information at the workstations, users may decide to leave the library, and they can easily do so because of the area's proximity to the entrance. A user's resources may be off-site, and perhaps an interlibrary transfer was requested through document delivery. At these workstations, a user may access and download information to a floppy disk, personal laptop computer, or notebook computer, and then move to a processing workstation located independently or in a laboratory while the full-access workstation is freed for another person.

In the electronic library, the reference and information services area becomes a center of high information-gathering activity, hardly the place to prepare results. Once basic sources are identified, CD-ROM full-text drafts retrieved, document-delivery requests placed, a user may retreat to another station to commence preparation of the end product—a term or research paper, annotated bibliography, or a compilation of technical information. From this point on, occasional assistance may be needed from technical staff but not from a librarian.

CONCLUSION

Effective information services will serve users both in the library and remote locations; this chapter focused on the services provided within a library building, and the outreach services were noted only in the figures. Power and communication links will assume a high level of importance; safeguarding them will be critical. The risks imposed by natural disturbances—ice storms, thunderstorms, temperature extremes causing stress on power supplies—will not be acceptable. Alternate power sources with instant recovery features will prove essential. To work out solutions will be challenging and time spent carefully reasoning each issue will be most beneficial.

ADDENDUM

Recently, I was involved in a preliminary planning study for the renovation of an academic library building. The objective was to determine the feasibility of renovating and expanding the building to accommodate the changing needs of the campus, but not to write a building program until after determining the opportunity for a successful project. If the study indicated the possibility of success at reasonable cost, then the project would proceed; if not, the potential for constructing a new building would be determined.

The building was deficient in its capability of supporting the necessary additional communication and power lines for the online workstations, which are needed to access in-house and outside information resources. The resolution of this problem would involve rewiring the building completely with category five, high-speed copper wiring and the extension of fiber-optic communication lines from the campus computer center. At that campus, the library building has no usable space for even a small computer installation; the air conditioning system is also marginal. This practical experience relates directly to this chapter and the material presented here was part of the planning study.

AN ELECTRONIC LIBRARY: A TEACHING LIBRARY

The College Library: An Assessment of Needs

For the advancement of library service, the college plans a construction/renovation project resulting in an electronic and teaching library that will serve for many years into the future. This document defines that concept and identifies some specific needs that, when fulfilled, will result in achieving the goal.

The electronic library is the next step in an evolutionary process from the traditional library to the networked library, to the electronic mode where most if not all of the library support is accessible through computers. This is partially achievable now as libraries progress from the partial network mode most are now in to a full network mode, and then to the electronic mode. The electronic library extends its influence and services to the home and far afield. Users, unconstrained by their location or library service hours, may access and retrieve resources immediately, identify some for later delivery, and send inquiries to reference and information services staff. Essentially, electronic information resources are always available. These include databases of statistical information, encyclopedic information, full-text journals and content tables, bibliographic information with and without abstracts, and graphic and artistic materials. Electronic and teaching library users, taught how to find and retrieve information, may have access to library resources from remote sites, or in the library through computer services supported by trained staff and other offline resources.

Learning begins in the classroom and develops further in the library where students are taught complex searching techniques by skilled librarians and staff for finding and using information sources held in the library or available from other repositories. Today, the generic term "workstation" describes a platform, a study carrel or table, equipped with a microcomputer terminal that provides the means for accessing online the holdings of the library, or computer-stored databases of information, or, through a network gateway, the resources of other libraries in this country and abroad. After intellectual stimulation in the classroom, students using the library are taught by librarians how to access additional information, how to interrelate various information carriers, whether held in computers, in media, or in print, and to build on the insights gained from their instructors. The teaching library continues the learning process begun by faculty in the classroom.

The finished facility will have workstations in the electronic mode, and the combination of classroom and library teaching and training will bring about the electronic and teaching library.

The college library will drive on the Information Highway through a regional gateway that allows access to the Internet, a major segment of the overall electronic information infrastructure now being developed. The availability of this high-speed telecommunications network makes the concept of an electronic and teaching library that supports the mission of the college and participates in the information superhighway feasible. Modifications to the existing library building will allow the delivery of high-quality, computer-based information services to students, faculty, and all communities in this geographic region. The college's outreach program, distance education, which provides educational opportunities to all people of its region, will benefit as well through the online delivery of information directly to students and faculty wherever located.

To achieve its goal, the library will need:

Staff: The concept involves a large public physical facility; a trained staff and certain requirements are necessary. Staff must have equipment for teaching and training novice users, accessing electronic resources, gathering and processing information, and organizing and codifying the electronic information resources (some of which may originate from the campus).

Collections: In this evolution, the academic library has accumulated resources in several formats of substantial value. To assure continuing usefulness, these require attention.

Design needs: An academic library building should have capabilities and features to support its mission. Some features are conducive and necessary to supporting and preserving the electronic equipment and collections.

Environment: Electronic equipment and material collections function and serve best with optimal air temperature, humidity, and quality.

Furniture and equipment: Electronic access equipment, which includes microcomputers, printers, disk drives, photocopiers, microform readers and printers, learning machines, and television devices, often requires platforms that differ from the traditional desk, table, or study carrel. In addition, because the library is a public building open to everyone, a wide range of other supporting furniture and equipment is necessary.

NOTES

1. Beginning with entry 10270, the 1994 Sweets catalog lists competitive products that will assist in providing power and communication connections and floor-raising systems, which permit elevations of less than three inches. These products are designed for office use in business and industry but are readily adaptable to library purposes. Service-outlet boxes that have connections for power, fiber-optic cables, and telephone lines are available. In installing raised floors, standards for access should be consulted if the floor will not be level with the entry. These guidelines are found in appendices B and C of the *Americans with Disabilities Act Handbook* (1991).

2. At the Association of College and Research Libraries conference held in Pittsburgh in March 1995, Jeff Heck and Gayle Baker presented a poster session about a scholar's workstation for a branch library. The printed packet supporting the poster session describes an electronic branch library. The project includes a plan to employ graduate students from the information sciences program to work as technical staff at each site 15 hours weekly (for more information, Heck can be reached at: 615–974–0087, or e-mail at: heck@utklib.lib.utk.edu).

REFERENCES

Americans with Disabilities Act Handbook. 1991. U.S. Equal Employment Opportunity Commission and the U.S. Dept. of Justice. Washington, D.C.: U.S. Government Printing Office.

Beckman, Margaret. 1990. ''Cost 'Avoidance' in Library Building Planning: What, Where, When, Why, Who?'' *Canadian Library Journal* (December): 405–409.

Cohen, Elaine. 1994. ''The Architectural and Interior Design Planning Process.'' *Library Trends* 42(3) (Winter): 547–563.

Heck, Jeff, and Gayle Baker. 1995. *The Scholar's Workstation Project: Testing a New Design for an Electronic Branch Library.* Knoxville: University of Tennessee.

Kaser, David. 1988. ''Academic Library Buildings: Their Evolution and Prospects.'' *Advances in Library Administration and Organization* 7: 149–160.

Martin, Murray S. 1994. ''Some Thoughts on the Future Academic Library.'' *Advances in Library Administration and Organization* 12: 85–108.

Sweet's General Building & Renovation Catalog File. 1994. Sweet's Group. New York: McGraw-Hill.

14

System Migration: A Bibliographic Essay

Catherine S. Cervarich

System migration is a fundamental aspect of library automation. It is the movement or changeover from one system or another. As online library systems become older, libraries are having to undergo the process of system migration. This migration can be either to an upgraded system from the same vendor or can be a change to an entirely different vendor. The issues involved in system migration are complex. This chapter will give several points of view to assist librarians about to begin this process. It will focus on general information about migration that is applicable to any library undergoing a migration—not the specifics only related to an individual case.

The literature on system migration can be divided into several broad categories: why libraries undergo migration; planning for migration; the use of consultants; technological considerations and processes of migration; the human and communication aspects of migration; migration as it relates specifically to serials; and experiences and sample accounts of migrations done by individual libraries. Many of the articles on migration overlap these broad categories.

According to a survey of 367 libraries, which have on online system that was installed in the last five years, conducted by Berry, "a whopping 58.5 percent of the public libraries and 40 percent of the college and university libraries have already upgraded their systems" (1989: 56). It is because of figures like these, and because of the number of libraries about to begin upgrading their systems, that information about system migration is important. In an article about the Norwalk Public Library migration from a network-based system to a stand-alone product, Jacob says, "System migration is a continuing process that reaffirms a library's automation commitment" (1991: 65). He adds that "system migration is central to library automation. . . . [Libraries] seek the advantages of emerging technologies at reduced costs." Library systems have a limited life span and according to Bridge, "attempts to extend system life to seven years usually sacrifice library credibility as system reliability decreases and service costs for older equipment escalate" (1992: 70).

Having said that system migration is an important, integral component of automation, how do you know when it is time to abandon your original system? According to Berry, most of the libraries that had already upgraded acquired the upgrade from their original vendor: "That left about 20 percent of the libraries willing to change systems rather than buy the upgrade from their current vendor" (1989: 56). Bridge (1992) suggests creating an advantage/disadvantage list about your current system. He stresses to be "brutally honest" during this process because you do not want to exchange your current problems and weaknesses for additional or more severe ones. On this list, write down your system's strengths and weaknesses on such topics as vendor support, adequacy of existing equipment, what is the current vendors "market prognosis," and what kind of libraries have purchased this system. If after doing this you have determined that your current system is inadequate, then you need to make the decision as to whether you need to upgrade your current system or change the entire system to a new vendor.

Pourciau conducted a survey of librarians to identify the similarities and differences associated with system migration in their libraries. He found ten main reasons that librarians gave for changing vendors: unresolved system problems; unacceptably long response times; obsolete hardware; a lack of confidence in the current vendor's future performance; abandonment of system of vendor; a new emphasis upon networking at the institutional level; an altered commitment by a parent institution to its library; an increasing sense by the library staff of the advanced age or dysfunctionality of its system in relation to the institution's system; attractiveness of new products offered by other vendors; and user complaints about system performance (1992: 106). Plank (1992) lists similar reasons why librarians changed vendors and also gives a time frame for the Request for Proposal (RFP) process.

Kershner (1992) discusses why librarians might want to upgrade with the same vendor. These reasons were: satisfaction with vendor performance; bypassing the time and cost of a formal RFP; avoiding the costs of replacement terminals; less extensive retraining of the library staff; and the expectation of an easier migration.

Planning is a major component of the process of successfully installing a new system. Plank discusses the importance of the planning and procuring process before the actual migration. She goes step-by-step from drafting the original RFP to awarding the contract to a vendor, placing each step of the process into an overall time frame. She emphasizes the importance of a "needs assessment" that examines the limitations of the current system including a statement of the problem (or problems) and the "anticipated results if resources are not acquired" (1991: 48). She discusses the various parts and stages of the RFP document. One of the most important aspects of the RFP is that with everything defined on paper, both the librarians and the vendor know exactly what the agreement includes.

Many librarians hire consultants to aid in the migration process. Epstein states the consultant's role in procurement is specially important, because the procurement of library systems is a complex, time-consuming, and expensive task. The consultant's role is to balance the needs and expectations of the librarians with those of the vendor so that the contract becomes a working document that both parties can live with. Epstein also discusses the context within which a negotiator typically works when preparing a contract. The four main parts of a contract are: "the body of the contract [that] contains the legal sections; a rider to the body that outlines a project schedule; a rider that outlines what will be acquired and how much it will cost; and a rider that outlines the testing that will occur to validate the performance of the contract" (1992b: 87). The consultant can assist the librarians in making decisions, but the final choices must remain theirs.

Cortez (1992) looks specifically at the role of the consultant during the development of the RFP. He discusses the origin of the RFP and contrasts the RFP with other procurement documents. He then discusses the many different roles that a consultant can play in the RFP process: teacher, advisor, assumption questioner, liaison, staff extension, clarifier, and system analyst. The type of role that the consultant plays "will depend on the experience of the library in procurement matters, the type of procurement, and the in-house resources available to the library" (1992: 97). Cortez concludes that the "library-consultant relationship is a partnership built on mutual trust and a reciprocal understanding of the roles each play in the procurement process" (1992: 97).

According to Newman, the growth and diversity of technology is changing rapidly and because of this, technical consultants play a special role in assisting this process. Newman states that "when hiring a consultant, you should assume that this is simply an additional staff member that has expert capabilities that you are in need of for a short-term assignment" (1992: 101). Next, Newman provides some case studies to demonstrate how to locate a consultant, what to ask for, and how to ensure that you get what you have requested.

Begg discusses the strengths that librarians and staff bring to a migration to a second system. First of all, they have previous automation experience, which enables them to ask more substantive and knowledgeable questions during the process. She states, "It is no doubt instructive to recall a first implementation when approaching a second one; but the more useful consideration is probably the implications of the existence of the first system at the moment the second system is to be brought into the library" (1991: 103). Begg also underscores the importance of planning and RFP development prior to system migration.

She stresses the importance of extensive site visits as the "single most inform-ative and decisive experience in the evaluation process the second time" (1992: 107). Through site visits, you can see how a system actually works in a library environment, without relying on what the vendor claims the system will do. In addition to migration planning, you will also need to begin implementation planning.

Epstein (1992a) discusses what libraries need to be aware of when they are considering a second system. She contrasts the differences between first and second system buyers and the changeover issues dealing with a second system, such as software license and proprietary information, bibliographic files, systems parameters, transition period, training, testing, and planning. Epstein stresses that automation is an ongoing process and not ever "finished."

The technological aspects of system migration has naturally received a lot of attention. What makes system migration different from your original automation project is the necessity of migrating data from the original system to the new system. This is one of the most difficult aspects of migrating.

Machovec explains what to look for in an integrated library system (ILS). He gives guidelines on technical issues for evaluating the systems available as sec-ond-generation ILS. He points out several issues to examine when considering a new system. "Integrated library systems are online transaction processing systems, and a hardware platform, which is optimized for this type of computer operation, will give improved performance. CPUs [central processing units], which can be enlarged or added to a modular basis without having to replace existing equipment, are desirable" (1991: 31). The system needs to be reliable with a "fault tolerant" hardware platform. "The ideal system will consist of multiple processors, dual interprocessor buses, dual-ported controllers, and mul-tiple power supplies" (1991: 31). Another feature that will improve system reliability is mirrored disk drives. All of this will maximize reliability but at very high costs. Connectivity must be designed into the new system. "High levels of performance and fast response time based on the experiences of sim-ilarly sized systems is crucial" (1991: 37). Librarians must also consider the costs for hardware, software, and maintenance as well as the ability to load multiple databases. Finally, consider flexible search software "which is menu-driven for novices and command-driven for experienced users" (1991: 39).

A useful outline of specific system requirements is provided by Millen et al. (1992). According to the authors, librarians should use the opportunity that a migration provides to take advantage of existing and potential software capa-bilities. Their outline of requirements describe an ideal online system with basic requirements, such as: types of databases that must be integrated into the system; types of search access points; search key and screen characteristics; printing options; are circulation, reserve, cataloging, acquisitions, and serials features. When purchasing a new system, keep in mind that trade-offs are often necessary. Millen et al. feel that the most important standards for library applications listed (this is in addition to the basic standards) are connectivity and interconnectivity.

Taylor also gives a listing of things to consider in outline form about hardware, software, and network issues during a migration. The outline includes the objectives of a conversion, hardware installation, network installation, software installation, and the actual "crunch time" when the migration takes place. Taylor states that the "vendor is the expert in conversions and should be made to assume the responsibility for anything that goes wrong" but that librarians must know their operations and "take the lead in establishing how the conversion will affect . . . operations" (1992: 170).

Sybrowsky discusses what type of data can be saved from the old system and sent to the new one. This includes CPU, peripheral hardware, application software, barcode labels, and various types of data files, such as bibliographic, patron, and transaction data. He then lists the ten steps that he feels will lead to a successful migration: analyze sample tapes or disks from all files that will need conversion; map out where the data contained on the tapes will be put in the new database; map out where all data needed by the new database will come from; write and test all programs to be used in the conversion process; load MARC data tapes and map the data into the bibliographic and item data files on the new system; load "static" patron data and have the library verify the data so far loaded; suspend operation of the current system; perform the final dump of data from the current system; and verify that the final data is loaded correctly (1991: 129–132).

Conversion program testing, argues Copeland, is a fundamental tool by which one "can assure the reliability and hence the quality of software" (1992: 166). She identifies and discusses those steps essential for a successful data conversion: writing specifications, testing, noting types of test data to be used, establishing a checklist of everything that needs to be reviewed and tested, performing error analysis, and terminating the test process. In addition, she states that librarians "should be aware of the types of testing conducted by the vendors and the vendors' previous experience with similar library software" (1992: 168).

Cortez and Smorch (1993) also provide excellent sources for technological information. Chapter four focuses on hardware platforms and software developments available for automated library systems. It examines and critiques several platforms and developments as well as the vendors associated with them. Chapter six discusses "importance of and sometimes difficulty with migrating the library's database." It gives the steps for database preparation, including datafile upgrades, tape tests to be conducted, time line for migration, authority control, and the management of the overall data migration process, from data conversion to handling patron files, reports, and statistics.

Warwick also discusses the data-mapping concerns during a migration. He stresses that the level of detail with which you document local library decisions and practice in your present system will affect the ease (or lack of ease) of later migration. He states that "consistency in implementing these local decisions and practices affects how accurately you can migrate data" (1994: 12).

The impact on the technical services staff is an aspect discussed by Wan in his account of one academic library's migration. In general, the major problem with migration is that the data in the earlier system does not always map directly to the new system. A "loader" program has to be written for the receiving system to make the data acceptable. Overall, this particular migration went well for technical services though "considerable time was spent subsequently to correct problems in serials and acquisitions" (1993: 20). It took two years to make the serials and acquisitions modules fully functional and for this reason, Wan calls for industrywide standards on serials and acquisitions so that any future migrations would be easier on the technical services staff.

McNutt (1992) discusses open systems options and strategies for migration. She speaks of the benefits that can be gained from open systems, so that a library would be positioned to take advantage of new technologies.

Epstein discusses a few legal concerns to keep in mind when migrating to a second system. She says that "the matter of the software license and vendor's proprietary information make it imperative to get your data off the original system" (1991: 76). The older vendor will have concerns about how the data from your original system is obtained in order to move it to the new system. Keep in mind that you need your current vendor until the second system is fully operational. Do extensive testing before the transfer takes place. One other thing to keep in mind is that often some statistics and year-to-date data may be lost; if possible, do the migration around the end or beginning of a fiscal year to minimize this problem.

Pastine and Kacena (1994) have written a bibliographic essay on budgeting and fund-raising requirements of automation. Budget requirements include obvious as well as hidden needs, one-time costs and ongoing costs. Some costs to considered include site preparation, conversion, implementation, training, and public relations. Because of these costs, budgeting considerations of automation need to be carefully addressed and considered.

There is also a human dimension that must be kept in mind when changing systems. Giesecke described the process of moving to a second-generation system using four frameworks of change: structural, human relations, political, and symbolic perspectives to analyze the process. She said, "The structural framework focuses on formal relationships, policies, and procedures that let the organization get things done. Human resources and relations focuses on improving employee motivation. The political framework concentrates on the competition for power and resources, and the symbolic framework focuses on rituals and meaning of work" (1992: 163). Using these frameworks to evaluate a migration, Giesecke underscored the importance of staff input, using staff recommendations, and giving people credit for ideas. This resulted in a general satisfaction with the system and the process.

Cronin also discusses using staff experience with automation to help the migration to a second system. She suggests involving the staff and providing staff training. Doing this will facilitate a smooth migration and "effective staff training is a primary ingredient of success" (1984: 76). In addition, she suggests creating the position of automation librarian, whose primary function would be staff training.

A few experts look specifically at serials system migration. Chiang (1994) discusses the planning and methodology of serials system migration at Queens College Library of the City University of New York, with special emphasis placed on the project design and the extensive use of programmed function keys. Function keys speeded up labor-intensive and repetitive data-input tasks, and helped staff members achieve maximum accuracy. She gives examples of the specific decisions reached and carefully discusses the reasoning behind each decision.

Banach (1993) discusses the serials system migration of 1989 by the University of Massachusetts at Amherst to a new system called Innopac. She discusses the original serials system and the difficulty of converting their serials holdings records. This difficulty was mainly because the holders were coded in a local format that predated the American National Standards Institute (ANSI) Z39.44 standard. In addition, she discusses the problems in converting the serial bibliographic records, which were not in MARC format and which were also incomplete. Many records predated the second edition of the *Anglo-American Cataloguing Rules* (AACR2). However, in spite of the problems, they were able to migrate the data successfully to a new serials database by combining data elements from two different sources. Doing so was difficult, but the end result was a smooth transition that was worth the effort.

Having looked at some specific aspects of system migration, where can one find good overall examples and samples of how systems migrations were done? Lach and Pattie (1992) produced an extremely helpful kit for those about to begin migration because it offers specific examples drawn from libraries that have already migrated. These examples include planning documents, workflow sheets, timetables, and public relations releases.

Another overall guide to the process of system migration is the book by Cortez and Smorch, which was mentioned earlier. In addition to the technological information given in chapters four and six, the book explains in detail how to do "the six major components to migration: assessment of library needs, planning and execution of the procurement process, relocation of the library's machine-readable files and handling of barcodes, the retirement or reutilization of existing equipment, installation and training, and testing and evaluation of system performance" (1993: 7). Above all, they suggest growing in use and file size when selecting a second system.

Hallmark and Garcia summarize the experiences of 33 libraries during migration. They describe successful experiences and "analyze mistakes, false assumptions, and delays to provide information and advice for those about to undertake a migration" (1992: 345). They discuss motivation for migration, planning for implementation, technical decisions and considerations, training, publicity, and relations with vendors. Some important advice is to communicate with and involve your staff, test in advance, give sufficient time for data transfer, hold the vendor to the dates promised, and try to keep everyone involved to be realistic. They also suggest to understand thoroughly how both the old and new systems handle and map data. Finally, if possible, run the old and new system in tandem for a while.

Carson (1993) discusses the experience of the Pennsylvania State University during its migration. This is an especially helpful place to look because of the extensive list of "hints" at the end of the article. She warns that any software bugs that have existed undetected on the old system will appear during migration.

The migration of Nene College in Northhampton, Massachusetts, is discussed in an article by Wilson (1994). He covers the rationale for migration, the vendor selection, the actual migration, and the problems encountered during the process. Like Carson's article, Wilson's provides a list of tips for those considering migration:

1. Do not expect a smooth transition, since there will be problems.

2. Negotiate a new contract and be particular about the specification for the number of concurrent users and the response time for the various functions.

3. Obtain a clear statement on system development issues and integrate these into the contract, if possible.

4. Employ the services of a good consultant to check every detail of your specifications and the company's migration proposal.

5. Mutually agree with your supplier to an analysis of peak transaction rates and have these monitored on-site against a declared checklist.

6. Have a detailed checklist for every aspect of functionality currently in use.

7. Measure the checklist against your old system. You will be surprised at the number of elements of your old system that are absent in the new.

8. Ensure that you have a project manager nominated by your system supplier with whom you can communicate daily.

9. Obtain a detailed breakdown of costs so that there are no "hidden extras" to surprise you.

10. Obtain an indication of potential upgrade paths.

11. Avoid whenever possible short-term "fixes" or contingency measures, which can give rise to further problems.

12. Invest heavily in training.

13. If system performance is not to your liking, insist on performance audits on site.

14. Operate on trust rather than mistrust of your system supplier.

An early migration experience is described in a two-part article by Kneedler (1988a, 1988b). He describes what set the stage for the Phoenix Public Library's migration project, including the reasons for the decision to migrate, the needs assessment for a new system, and the writing, revising, and issuing of the request for procurement. He discusses the process of selecting a new system and the actual migration. Kneedler highlights the problems and accomplishments encountered during this migration. He points out that the Phoenix Public Library was one of the first large public libraries to migrate when "methodologies for migration were still in their infancy." He covers the vendor selection process, moving the data, the installation, training and cutover, and staff satisfaction (and overexpectation) at the end of the project. Kneedler candidly admits to major problems caused by earlier database entry errors and inconsistencies, which hampered moving the data from the old system to the new one.

Smith and Borgendale provide a framework for decisions and actions in the process of converting from one online system to another. They emphasize the practical consideration of migration in order to help libraries anticipate what is needed to migrate and to help with the "writing of the RFP and the subsequent procurement and installation of the new system" (1988: 47). They discuss technical considerations of migration, management issues, planning, profiling, user interface issues, datafile conversion training, and the conversion process.

In reviewing the literature available, two terms appeared repeatedly—planning and communication. According to the experts, these are the most important factors in migration. If you have a detailed plan and free flow of communication to and from the staff, the migration to a second system should go smoothly. Plan each phase of the migration process and involve your staff in both the planning and the execution. These efforts will make for a more successful migration.

REFERENCES

Banach, Patricia S. 1993. "Migration from an In-house Serials System to Innopac at the University of Massachusetts at Amherst." *Library Software Review* 12 (Spring): 35–37.

Begg, Karin. 1991. "Putting It All Together and Making It Work." In *Library Systems Migration: Changing Automated Systems in Libraries and Information Centers*, ed. Gary M. Pitkin. Westport, Conn.: Meckler, pp. 102–123.

Berry, John N. 1989. "Upgrading Systems, Software, and Microcomputers." *Library Journal* 114 (September 15): 56–59.

Bridge, Frank R. 1992. "System Migration: Abandoning Your Vendor." *Library Journal* 177 (May): 68–70.

Carson, Sylvia Mackinnon. 1993. "Library Information Access System at the Pennsylvania State University: A Migration Story." In *Insider's Guide to Library Automation: Essays of Practical Experience*, eds. John W. Head and Gerard B. McCabe. Westport, Conn.: Greenwood Press, pp. 31–42.

Chiang, Belinda. 1994. "Migration from Microlinx to NOTIS: Expediting Serials Holding Conversion Through Programmed Function Keys." *Serials Librarian* 25 (January–February): 115–131.

Copeland, Nora S. 1992. "Testing Data Migration." In *Information Technology: It's for Everyone: Proceedings of the LITA Third National Conference*, ed. Thomas W. Leonhardt. Chicago: American Library Association, pp. 166–168.

Cortez, Edwin M. 1992. "The Use of Consultants in the Development of Request for Proposals." In *Using Consultants in Libraries and Information Centers: A Management Handbook*, ed. Edward D. Garten. Westport, Conn.: Greenwood Press, pp. 91–98.

Cortez, Edwin M., and Tom Smorch. 1993. *Planning Second Generation Automated Library Systems*. Westport, Conn.: Greenwood Press.

Cronin, Mary J. 1984. "The Second Time Around: Transition to a New Integrated Library System." *Library Hi Tech* 7 (April): 76–77.

Epstein, Susan Baerg. 1991. "Implementing a Second System: Some New Concerns." *Library Journal* 116 (January): 76–77.

———. 1992a. "Planning for Second Systems: An Introduction." In *Information Technology: It's for Everyone: Proceedings of the LITA Third National Conference*, ed. Thomas W. Leonhardt. Chicago: American Library Association, pp. 146–148.

———. 1992b. "The Role of the Consultant in Contract Negotiations: Expectations, Responsibilities, and Limitations." In *Using Consultants in Libraries and Information Centers: A Management Handbook*, ed. Edward D. Garten. Westport, Conn.: Greenwood Press, pp. 83–89.

Giesecke, Joan. 1992. "Post-implementation Blues: Managing the Transition to a Second System." In *Information Technology: It's for Everyone: Proceedings of the LITA Third National Conference*, ed. Thomas W. Leonhardt. Chicago: American Library Association, pp. 163–165.

Hallmark, Julie, and C. Rebecca Garcia. 1992. "System Migration: Experience from the Field." *Information Technology and Libraries* 11 (December): 345–357.

Jacob, William. 1991. "System Migration: Bettering Tomorrow Today." In *Proceedings of the Sixth Integrated Online Library Systems Meeting*, ed. David C. Genaway. Medford, N.J.: Learned Information, pp. 65–72.

Kershner, Lois M. 1992. "Upgrade with Same Vendor." In *Information Technology: It's for Everyone: Proceedings of the LITA Third National Conference*, ed. Thomas W. Leonhardt. Chicago: American Library Association, pp. 149–150.

Kneedler, William H. 1988a. "The Phoenix Public Library Migration Part I: The Birth and Death of an Early System." *Online Libraries and Microcomputers* 6 (November): 1–5.

———. 1988b. "The Phoenix Public Library Migration Part II: Selecting a New System Migration." *Online Libraries and Microcomputers* 6 (December): 1–11.

Lach, Michael, and Ling-yuh W. Pattie. 1992. *System Migration in ARL Libraries* (SPEC Kit), ed. C. Brigid Welch. Washington D.C.: Association of Research Libraries, Office of Management Services.

Machovec, George S. 1991. "The Technology of Change: What's Involved and How It Is Accomplished." In *Library Systems Migration: Changing Automated Systems in Libraries and Information Centers*, ed. Gary M. Pitkin. Westport, Conn.: Meckler, pp. 30–47.

McNutt, Dinah. 1992. "Administering the Migration to Unix." *Unix Review* 10 (March): 31–37.

Millen, Celeste, D. Ron Johnson, Roger Lowery, and Joanna Wright. 1992. *Outline of Standards for Migration to Integrated Online System*. Wilmington: University of North Carolina. ERIC, ED 349–009.

Newman, Wilda B. 1992. "Using Consultants to Evaluate and Strengthen Systems and Computing Resources: Case Studies from a Large Research Organization." In

Using Consultants in Libraries and Information Centers: A Management Handbook, ed. Edward D. Garten. Westport, Conn.: Greenwood Press, pp. 99–110.

Pastine, Maureen, and Carolyn Kacena. 1994. "Library Automation, Networking, and Other Online and New Technology Costs in Academic Libraries." *Library Trends* 42 (Winter): 524–536.

Plank, Marietta A. 1991. "The Implementation of Change: Planning and the RFP Process." In *Library Systems Migration: Changing Automated Systems in Libraries and Information Centers*, ed. Gary M. Pitkin. Westport, Conn.: Meckler, pp. 48–68.

———. 1992. "Changing Vendors for a Next-generation Library System." In *Information Technology: It's for Everyone: Proceedings of the LITA Third National Conference*, ed. Thomas W. Leonhardt, Chicago: American Library Association, pp. 151–152.

Pourciau, Lester J. 1992. "Automated Library System Migration in the United States." *Electronic Library* 10 (April): 103–108.

Smith, Barbara G., and Marilyn Borgendale. 1988. "The Second Time Around: The Next Generation Local Online System." *Library Journal* 113 (July): 47–51.

Sybrowsky, Paul K. 1991. "A Vendor's Perspective: Dynix on System Migrations." In *Library Systems Migration: Changing Automated Systems in Libraries and Information Centers*, ed. Gary M. Pitkin. Westport, Conn.: Meckler, pp. 124–133.

Taylor, Jim. 1992. "Hardware, Software, and Network Issues During Second System Installations." In *Information Technology: It's for Everyone: Proceedings of the LITA Third National Conference*, ed. Thomas W. Leonhardt: Chicago: American Library Association, pp. 169–170.

Wan, William W. 1993. "System Migration and Its Impact on Technical Services." *Public Library Quarterly* 13(4) 13–20.

Warwick, Robert T. 1994. "Moving to a New Automated System: Some Issues." *New Jersey Libraries* 27 (Spring): 11–14.

Wilson, Maurice. 1994. "Talis at Nene: An Experience in Migration in a College Library." *Program* 28 (July): 239–251.

15

Managing the Integrated Library System

Rhonda Ames

The Integrated Library System (ILS) has become the model for almost all institutionally based library automation activities. Lynch (1991) defines the basic concept of the ILS as, "a single system with a common database, which supported the full range of library automation functions, ranging from acquisitions to circulation to the public access online catalog, using a single integrated database." Beginning with the development of these systems in the early 1980s he provides an excellent overview of the evolution within the context of the environmental factors that have shaped current ILSs. In response to the "networking access revolution" occurring in the late 1980s, a modern ILS is expected to interact with many other institutional data-processing centers (Online Public Access Catalogs, Online Computer Library Center, and Current Contents, to name a few). Access to a multitude of networked resources has raised user expectations far beyond the local catalog that was the standard in the 1980s. A modern ILS must support electronic downloading of text, accommodate varying hardware and software platforms, and provide a uniform user-friendly interface to a complex array of electronic resources. The intent of this chapter is to provide an overview of the organizational patterns for ILS administration and the key requirements for successful ILS management.

In the majority of academic libraries, an ILS exists. In fact, many institutions are planning second- or third-generation systems. A given is that any system will require expansion and modification over time. Due to the geometric progression of technological developments and corresponding user expectations, today's system is but a prototype of the system that will evolve in five years. Schappert presents compelling reasons for viewing library automation projects as ongoing, and not as a process with a definite beginning, middle, and end. In describing the various ways that libraries have handled the administration of library systems, she recommends "However it is accomplished, some individual needs to monitor routines and participate, with some vision, in the evolution of the automated library" (1993: 262).

Who are the people responsible for managing a library system? Martin (1988) examines the relationship of the library and its information provision function to system librarians—who are the people who identify the needs of the library for automated systems, cause these systems to be implemented, and analyze the operations of the library. Summarizing a 1986 Association of Research Libraries report of organization charts (SPEC Kit 129) of 86 libraries that each have a systems librarian tells us the following: in most cases the role and responsibilities of these systems librarians are restricted to the automation of existing library procedures or to implementing an online catalog. What system librarians currently are defined as doing, implementing and maintaining systems, is contrasted with what system librarians need to do: remain current with evolving technologies, maintain working relationships with computing center staff, provide staff support for online bibliographic databases and CD-ROM use, and develop online bibliographic databases. Parkhurst (1990) commenting on the same 1986 ARL report notes that all but seven of the libraries reviewed had some type of unit designated to deal with and be responsible for automation.

In another survey (Epstein 1991) of public, academic, consortia, and special libraries that had purchased Dynix as either turn-key or software-only systems, the typical inventory of job duties included system hardware maintenance, weekly backup of the system, peripheral troubleshooting and repairs, and new employee training. Most held MLS degrees and acquired the necessary expertise on the job, thus becoming system administrators from promotion within the organization or by default. The amount of time spent on system duties averaged eleven hours per week, with each individual's time dependent on the size of the system and its implementation status.

Leonard (1993) found that the three main categories of tasks performed by system librarians are planning, installation, and maintenance. The most time-consuming responsibility was microcomputer maintenance, especially CD-ROM and LAN maintenance. According to Leonard, this indicated a move away from mainframe systems toward distributed computing environments. Perhaps the most apropos of statements characterizing the duties and functions of the system librarian can be found in the article by Muirhead (1993: 124): "The post of the system librarian is an often unpredictable cocktail of duties, determined as much by the conditions and constraints [that] operate at a local level as by any universally agreed model of what a system librarian should do."

Articles written by system administrators describe either the various duties performed or the functions served by the library's system department. Crawford

(1991) discusses his responsibilities as the system administrator in a small liberal arts college in New Jersey as well as the advantages and disadvantages or a public service librarian fulfilling the dual role of reference service and online system administrator.

White, acquisitions librarian turned automation librarian, describes the many functions he performs and the variety of personal computer applications that he implemented in a medium-sized federal library. He states: "Even libraries with totally integrated systems will need to use PCs to fill in the gaps with in-house designed and developed PC applications" (White 1990: 257). Additional suggestions for the library director to keep in mind are: (1) automation librarians are usually not professional programmers; (2) require high-quality proposals from your automation librarian; (3) provide backup support for your automation librarian; (4) be an informed manager (so if your automation librarian left tomorrow, you would be able to maintain the system).

Individuals in the academic reference department at the University of Arizona, tired of having to remember the command languages of the more than 40 different systems in the department, decided that responsibilities for the various automated systems should be distributed among all members of the reference department (Johnson 1991). This illustrates what can be accomplished by collaborative efforts among colleagues.

THE LIBRARY AND THE ACADEMIC COMPUTING CENTER

A recurring topic in the literature reviewed involves the relationship between the librarian and the university computing center. All but one of the libraries noted in this chapter have formal or informal ties with computing centers either administratively or operationally.

Quinlan illustrates the parallel roles played by academic computing centers and libraries, noting that the common ground between them is the technology they use: "Computation is being done less on single large computers and more on smaller diffuse systems of machines, just as the concept of the library as a single building filled with books is changing to one of a diffuse base of widely accessible information" (1991: 96). Another common purpose is that both professions want to enhance the organization and accessibility of information available on campus. Computing professionals tend to view information on a more symbolic level—as data to be manipulated, stored, and transmitted—whereas library professionals are concerned with the content and presentation of information. Success in such a technology-based environment requires that we computing professionals and library professionals work together.

In her account of developing an automated library system, Yoshikawa (1993) offers an amusing and pragmatic view of the issues involved in managing an on-site library system. This librarian, with a computer science background, developed the Hillsborough Community College's library system and lists fundamental points learned from her experiences; three, in particular, are relevant: (1) you need administrative support, (2) you need a technical-support person, and (3) you need a software-support person.

Stephens, library director of the Stern Library at the University of Birmingham, discusses the pros and cons of having an on-site computing center managed by the library or, depending on the university, the computing center. He asserts, "The major advantage of a library computing center is that the system itself is under the direct control of the library administration" (1993: 313). Other advantages include: the ability to implement changes and enhancements specifically tailored for library purposes; greatly increased processing time gained by not having to compete with other departments for computer resources; and increased staff participation and insight into the direct operation of the system. Although considerations of data security, application functionality, and database integrity are just a few of the ongoing concerns involved in maintaining a system, this director believes that the advantages of assuming the responsibilities for all aspects of the library system far outweigh the disadvantages.

Some academic libraries and computing centers are combining the talents of both professions into one organizational structure responsible for campus-wide information provision. In 1991 the Library Information Technologies (LIT) structure was formed at Case Western Reserve University. Positive aspects of this collaboration include validation of each unit's concerns of service and equipment needs, librarians' better understanding of technological capabilities, and an increased service awareness within computing. Negative aspects include possible loss of autonomy and control, of either profession's priorities, and of balance between planning for the future and providing for today. Metz claims, "Bringing the two groups of professionals together organizationally can work, but *working* together and not organizational structure is the key" (1991: 99). A similar relationship exists between MIT's information systems and library: "The cooperative model is clearly a viable alternative.... Given the complexity and magnitude of the issues involved, we are extremely fortunate to have developed an excellent working relationship and a strong sense of mutual confidence and respect" (Lucker 1993: 86). Lynch (1994) presents an overview of the information technology section of the Albert R. Mann Library at Cornell University. The focus is on its key role regarding public services, technical services and preservation, and collection development. Six functions are discussed: maintainer, interpreter, trainer, enabler, liaison, and advisor.

ORGANIZATIONAL STRUCTURE

Weber (1988) focuses on the question of how to achieve the most effective application of computer information technology to university library services. He states that the "organizational dilemma" involves three principle components: (1) the traditional library organization; (2) the Information Technology Organization (ITO), which includes the computer center; and (3) the office providing coordination over the first two. Using Stanford University's ITO as an example, he traces how one university has addressed the problem of the organizational dilemma. In the ITO model, the relationship of the library to the ITO is through the coordination of processes rather than through the assignment of personnel or operational control of library units (i.e., the libraries and Information Resource Organization work collaboratively on all connected technological systems within Stanford University's libraries).

Flower defines telecommunications information policy as "the plan or course of action adopted by a university, designed to influence and determine decisions and actions regarding the communication of information and knowledge via the transmission of signals, through voice, data, or video communication systems" (1987: 93). In order to evaluate how telecommunications information policy issues are resolved on campus by the existing organizational structures, and the role of the library and university computing facilities in the formation of telecommunications policies, Flower conducted a survey of 26 American Research Libraries. He identifies and discusses four organizational structures or models: (1) the academic affairs model; (2) administrative services model; (3) computing/information systems (CIS) model; and (4) the decentralized model, which includes a committee-based model. It was determined that library involvement in policy formation was limited and the relationship between libraries and computing facilities is founded on practical needs rather than future possibilities. Flower concludes by stating that the library and computing facilities must be directly involved in telecommunications technology policy formation; failure to do so is sure to create inefficiencies and great expense over time.

CONCLUSION

Each of the libraries considered in this chapter has developed its own unique solution for managing a library system. What is evident from the literature is that the function and role of the integrated library system administrator is evolving in as complex and unique ways as automation systems. A complex set of options and decisions face any library system administrator. Integrating all the effective components of automated library system into one seamless whole—greater than the sum of its parts—requires long-range planning guided by a clear understanding of the needs of the user community. Montague offers the following advice: "[It] is essential that library management plan for a true integration of automated capabilities across functions, ask hard questions about the long-term cost-benefit trade-off of decisions, question historical sacred cows, establish effective communication links with staff, and take a more aggressive role in shaping capabilities, schedules, and priorities in future network and national planning developments" (1993: 85).

Managing an ILS implementation of any type is not trivial. Because of the complexities in administering an ILS, it is imperative that at least one person be responsible for the management and maintenance of the system. All libraries reviewed had at least one individual responsible for system management, although the duties varied from site to site depending upon local policies and environment. Furthermore, the emphasis was toward developing in-house expertise and maintaining local control of the system. In those situations where a staff member was given the responsibility of managing the ILS in addition to his or her preexisting duties, the extra time and effort needed to properly manage the system was difficult, if not impossible, to achieve. Finally, cooperation with the computing center is essential. All of the libraries have operational links with university computing centers. The technical issues involved in linking to external resources such as the Internet, bibliographic utilities, and campus local area networks, require the expertise of those trained in computer and telecommunications technologies. In this way, both the library and the computing center benefit from a cooperative and congenial relationship.

REFERENCES

Crawford, Gregory A. 1991. "The Public Services Librarian As System Administrator." In *Proceedings of the Sixth Integrated Online Library Systems Meeting*, ed. David C. Genaway. Medford, N.J.: Learned Information, pp. 33–38.

Epstein, Susan Baerg. 1991. "Administrators of Automated Systems: A Survey." *Library Journal* 116 (July 15): 56–57.

Flower, Kenneth E. 1987. "Academic Libraries on the Periphery: How Telecommunications Information Policy Is Determined in Universities." *Journal of Library Administration* 8 (Summer): 93–107.

Johnson, Ralph N. 1991. "Managing Automation Through Distributed Responsibilities: An Academic Reference Department Model." *Library Software Review* 10 (July–August): 275–276.

Leonard, Barbara G. 1993. "The Role of the Systems Librarian/Administrator: A Preliminary Report." *Library Administration & Management* 7(2): 113–116.

Lucker, Jay K. 1993. "Sidebar 1: Relationships." *Library Hi Tech* 11(1): 86.

Lynch, Clifford A. 1991. "The System Perspective." In *The Evolution of Library Automation: Management Issues and Future Perspectives*, ed. Gary M. Pitkin. Westport, Conn.: Meckler, pp. 39–57.

Lynch, Tim. 1994. "The Many Roles of an Information Technology Section." *Library Hi Tech* 12(3): 38–43.

Martin, Susan K. 1988. "The Role of the Systems Librarian." *Journal of Library Administration* 9(4): 57–68.

Metz, Ray E. 1991. "Library and Computing Staff: Learning from One Another." In *Proceedings of the Sixth Integrated Online Library Systems Meeting*, ed. David C. Genaway. Medford, N.J.: Learned Information, pp. 97–102.

Montague, Eleanor. 1993. "Automation and the Library Administrator." *Information Technology and Libraries* 12 (March); reprinted from *Journal of Library Administration* 11 (December 1978): 313–323.

Muirhead, Graeme A. 1993. "The Role of the Systems Librarian in Libraries in the United Kingdom." *Journal of Librarianship and Information Science* 25 (September): 123–125.

Parkhurst, Carol A. 1990. "The In-house Expert: The Role of the Systems Librarian." *Library Software Review* 9 (March–April): 96–97.

Quinlan, Catherine A. 1991. "Libraries and Computing Centers." In *The Evolution of Library Automation: Management Issues and Future Perspectives*, ed. Gary M. Pitkin. Westport, Conn.: Meckler, pp. 91–103.

Schappert, Catherine H. 1993. "The Library Automation Project: Is It Ever Really Done?" In *Insider's Guide to Library Automation: Essays of Practical Experience*, eds. John W. Head and Gerard B. McCabe. Westport, Conn.: Greenwood Press, pp. 261–271.

Stephens, Jerry W. 1993. "Computer Center or Library Director: Is There a Choice?" In *Insider's Guide to Library Automation; Essays of Practical Experience*, eds. John W. Head and Gerard B. McCabe. Westport, Conn.: Greenwood Press, pp. 307–314.

Weber, David C. 1988. "University Libraries and Campus Information Technology: Who Is in Charge Here?" *Journal of Library Administration* 9(2): 5–19.

White, Frank. 1990. "The Role of the Automation Librarian in the Medium-sized Library." *Canadian Library Journal* 47 (August): 257–267.

Yoshikawa, Viveca. 1994. "Library Automation . . . by Trial and Error." In *Insider's Guide to Library Automation: Essays of Practical Experience*, ed. John W. Head and Gerard B. McCabe. Westport, Conn.: Greenwood Press, pp. 43–49.

Index

About the Editors and Contributors

JOHN W. HEAD is Associate Professor in the library science department at Clarion University of Pennsylvania, and has worked in public and academic libraries. A member of the American Library Association and the Pennsylvania Library Association, he is interested in information retrieval, library automation, and research methods.

GERARD B. McCABE was director of libraries at Clarion University of Pennsylvania. He is the editor of *Operations Handbook for the Small Academic Library* (Greenwood Press, 1989), *Academic Libraries in Urban and Metropolitan Areas: A Management Handbook* (Greenwood Press, 1992), *Insider's Guide to Library Automation* (Greenwood Press, 1993), *Academic Libraries: Their Rationale and Role in American Higher Education* (Greenwood Press, 1995).

RHONDA AMES has a B.S.C.S. and an M.S.L.S. from Clarion University of Pennsylvania. In the past she has worked as a programmer for Pinellas Park Public Library and is currently Access Services Coordinator for Ohio Valley Public Libraries.

CASSANDRA BRUSH has been the system librarian at the Pittsburgh Theological Seminary for the last four years. Her previous experience includes a four-year term as head of technical services for a small four-year college in

Pennsylvania, senior technical consultant for Brodart's automated systems, bibliographic services coordinator for the California Spanish Language Database, and cataloger at California State College at Hayward, California. She wrote articles in the proceedings of the IOLS meeting held annually in New York for four consecutive years, and teaches "Management of Library Automation" at the University of Pittsburgh's School of Library and Information Science.

PAUL F. BURTON is a senior lecturer in the Department of Information Science of the University of Strathclyde, Glasgow, Scotland. He teaches a wide range of courses and is interested in the effect of information technologies at all levels, with particular reference to the "virtual library" concept, electronic journals, and electronic mail. He is the author of *Information Technology and Society* (1992), has published many articles in professional journals, and has presented material at conferences in Britain, Europe, and Japan.

CATHERINE S. CERVARICH is a former library science graduate student at Clarion University of Pennsylvania.

STEPHEN P. FOSTER is director of technical services at Central Michigan University Library. He has worked in library technical services as a law librarian, an OCLC network librarian, and as a cataloging department head. He has an M.L.S. from Western Michigan University and a Ph.D. from St. Louis University.

NANCY C. FRICKE has school, public, and university library experience. Most recently she has been a librarian in the cataloging department at Indiana University of Pennsylvania, where she was responsible for database management.

HOWARD GRAVES is systems librarian and catalog department chairperson in the Joan and Donald E. Azinn Library of Hofstra University. He received a B.A. from Bucknell University, an M.L.S. from the Palmer Graduate School of Library and Information Science at Long Island University, and an M.A. from Hofstra University.

MARYHELEN JONES is director of Central Michigan University's Off-Campus Library Services. In her twenty-year career as a library practitioner and administrator, she has held both public and technical services positions in academic, corporate, government, and public libraries. Ms. Jones received an M.L.S. from the University of North Carolina at Chapel Hill.

MYRTLE JOSEPH is a cataloging and reference librarian at Indiana University of Pennsylvania. She is a graduate of the Catholic University of America's School of Library and Information Sciences. Her research interests include library automation and workflow management. She is currently investigating the feasibility of telecommuting cataloging.

SUSAN E. KETCHAM is a cataloger at the Long Island University Library, Southampton, New York.

TOM KLINGLER is head of reference at The University of Akron, Ohio.

TERRENCE F. MECH is vice president for information and instructional technologies and director of the library at King's College in Wilkes-Barre, Pennsylvania. He holds a D.Ed. in higher education from the Pennsylvania State University.

MELANIE J. NORTON is an assistant professor of library and information sciences at the University of Southern Mississippi in Hattiesburg, Mississippi. She has been involved in computer network and information management as a librarian and systems manager since 1981.

ELAINE SANCHEZ received her B.A. in German and M.L.S. from the University of Texas at Austin. She has been head of cataloging at Southwest Texas State University since 1987.

MARGARET SYLVIA is the assistant director for technical services at St. Mary's University Academic Library in San Antonio. She is a reviewer for *Library Journal* and *Library Software Review.* She has published a number of articles on computer networks in libraries as well as on collection development.

CHRISTINE E. THOMPSON is head of the cataloging department at the University of Alabama Library. Dr. Thompson holds an M.L.S. from the University of North Texas and a Ph.D. from Texas Woman's University. She is a frequent contributor to professional journals and is a regular reviewer for both *ARBA* and *The Armchair Detective.*

JUDITH TIERNEY is head of reference at King's College, Wilkes-Barre, Pennsylvania.

JENNIFER L. WALZ is assistant reference librarian at King's College, Wilkes-Barre, Pennsylvania. She serves as coordinator of the library's CD-ROM network.

RICK WIGGINS is network project leader for the computing center at The University of Akron, Ohio.